WHAT'S NEXT

WHAT'S NEXT

YOUR DREAM JOB, GOD'S CALL, AND A LIFE THAT SETS YOU FREE

DANIEL RYAN DAY

Discovery House.
from Our Daily Bread Ministries

Discovery House is affiliated with Our Daily Bread Ministries, Grand Rapids, Michigan.

Requests for permission to quote from this book should be directed to: Permissions Department, Discovery House, PO Box 3566, Grand Rapids, MI 49501, or contact us by email at permissionsdept@dhp.org.

Interior design by Beth Shagene

ISBN: 978-1-62707-943-3

Printed in the United States of America

First printing in 2019

To Rebecca, my love.
At least when we ask, "What's next?"
we do it together, hand in hand.
It's not as scary a question when you ask it with me.

And to the team at Asheville's Fun Depot—
this book is written for you.

CONTENTS

INTRODUCTION

Searching for your next step in life can be exciting yet overwhelming, intriguing yet stressful, adventurous yet painful. "What's next?" is a question everyone asks and struggles with at some point in his or her life, and many people end up asking this question multiple times. I have a friend who's 18 and trying to figure out if he should go to college or not. I have another friend who's 21 and can't decide what major to choose. I work with some people who are graduating from college and are taking their first step toward a career. I just got off the phone with someone I deeply care about who's trying to keep his dream afloat while also paying the bills. All of these men and women are asking, "What's next?" All are searching for answers.

For some of us, "What's next?" is a question of dreams—What could the future look like if I did this or that? There's an excitement that comes with thinking about all the possibilities and potential. For others, the question is stressful, and the answer may require a major transition, like moving away from family or changing jobs. Thinking about the future carries with it equal amounts of angst and anticipation. "What's next?"

always ventures into the unknown. If you're asking "What's next?"—join the club! You're not alone.

This book is for dreamers and practicalists (no, this is not a real word, but it should be). It's for those who are excited about transition and those who dread it. It's a book about the hope and freedom that comes with asking God what He wants for your life, and then hearing His voice through the pages of Scripture as He directs your steps.

As we begin this journey together, here's my prayer: "Give us eyes to see and ears to hear your voice, Lord. Speak; your servants are listening."

1

WHAT'S NEXT?

I never imagined I would be thirty years old and still trying to figure out who I wanted to be when I grew up.

As a boy, I thought for sure I would fly F-16s. It's all I wanted to do with my life. I was so serious about it that I built control panels out of Legos, commandeered the joystick from my parents' computer, and set up my bed as a cockpit. I flew thousands of missions all over the world. I don't mean to brag, but I was the best fighter pilot ever to maneuver a four-poster bed.

As I got older, my desire to fly airplanes only grew stronger. When I turned seventeen, I contacted my congressman, and he agreed to write a recommendation letter for my acceptance into the United States Air Force Academy. Unless you're a really bad student with a criminal record, a letter from a congressman almost always guarantees acceptance into the Academy. So I was set.

Before I sent in my application, however, I met a cute little

Cuban girl and fell in love. Suddenly, the thought of moving out of state to attend the Air Force Academy sounded terrible, so I never sent in the application. Instead, I went to a local university, and Rebecca and I were married a few years later.

My desire to fly hadn't gone away though. In fact, a few months before our wedding, I met with an Air Force recruiter to check out the process of becoming a pilot without going through the Academy. Providentially, he was a terrible recruiter, and I left the meeting without any peace about the possibility of becoming an Air Force pilot. Rebecca wisely reminded me that God is a God of peace, and she encouraged me to pay attention when my heart is in turmoil.

I tried a different route. I contacted my uncle, who had flown missionary planes for the Jungle Aviation and Radio Service for fifty years. He advised me about what it would take to become a missionary pilot, and soon I was accepted by a university that specialized in the type of training I would need. But again, I didn't feel peace. Instead of changing colleges, I finished my business degree at the local university.

And then I entered the workforce. Over the next few years, however, whenever my job became difficult or stressful, I felt a burning in my chest to abandon everything and jump into a cockpit. I got to the point where I felt that if I didn't become a pilot, I could never be content in any other job.

What is it that fuels that discontent?

IN TRANSITION

I'm now 100 percent certain that I'm not supposed to become a professional pilot, and I've lost all desire to go into the Air Force, but contentment was still elusive for a long time. The idea of watching the sun rise and set from high above the earth sounded so beautiful and adventurous. It sounded like the perfect dream job. What else could I do that would be as great as flying a fighter jet?

"What's next?" was constantly on my mind. And I've since discovered that it's on lots of people's minds.

Right now, I manage a restaurant and family entertainment center—the kind with go-carts, laser tag, mini golf, and an arcade. Our family-owned business employs about sixty people, and I would say the majority of our staff are "in transition." They are like you: some know exactly what their dream job is, some have no idea, and some are simply searching for the next step in their education or career. Some are students and young adults, and some are men and women in their thirties, forties, and older who are searching for something better. These folks are looking for what's next, but they may not know what that looks like.

If the people who work with me were divided into "teams" based on where they're at in life, we'd see their diversity. Maybe you can relate to one of them . . .

The first team is Team Senior, and no, I'm not talking about those ages sixty-five and up who get free coffee at restaurants. These are young adults who are trying to figure out what's next after high school. If you're in this group, you may have applied to a few colleges or universities and are anxiously awaiting answers. Or you may have already decided on a college but still have no idea what your major will be. You could also be in this group if you've decided to take a break from school until you know for sure what you want to do with your life. Either way, you are asking—or at least thinking about—"what's next" and would really like to know the answer. It's also possible someone who really cares may have purchased this book for you because they want you to begin thinking and dreaming about your future. That's great because you'll get a head start on one of the biggest questions people face in their lives and, if you take this search seriously, you can avoid a lot of the trouble the rest of us have experienced.

Team College is next, and it's diverse. There are those who, like I did, are bouncing—with much stress (and possibly whiplash)—from major to major. If that's you, you probably expected to have your goals figured out by now, and are frustrated that your "what's next" is still "What major should I choose?" You could also be on Team College if you're approaching the end of your studies, and the guaranteed job you thought you'd have is not as guaranteed as you thought. The timeline in your head included a job offer before graduation. Now graduation is closing in—or has already passed—and you don't have any promising prospects. You're still working at a burger joint, and the question "what's next" means "When and where is my career going to start?" This is such a difficult place to be.

I've had many friends on Team Rut because they feel like they're, well, in a rut. If that's you, maybe you took a break between high school and college to figure out what career field to pursue, but now years have passed and you're still cleaning public bathrooms or running a cash register. Or you may have what many people consider a good job—steady work, regular raises, vacation—but you're bored; it feels like a dead end. Either way, you may still ask "what's next" every once in a while, but you may have given up hope on ever finding the answer.

Team Bills is a really large group! They understand the need for an income and are humble enough to take whatever job they can get to pay their bills. I've had some incredibly overqualified people work for us who took the job to make ends meet while getting back on their feet. If that's you, you are probably happy to have a job, but are still eager to find "what's next"—especially because you know that you have so much more to offer.

Team Deck-of-Cards includes people who have been dealt a rough hand through their own decisions, the decisions of others, or circumstances outside of their control. Maybe you had a dream career that you were pursuing, but a sudden death, divorce, job loss, or illness ravaged your plans, your emotions, and your life. Now you're floundering and questioning God. Maybe you're working for an hourly wage at the only job you could find while you try to put the pieces back together. I can only imagine how personal the question "what's next" is for you.

Finally, there's Team Hero—the few people I know who have purposefully given up on a dream to become an unsung hero for someone they care about. Maybe the situation caused you to take on responsibility before you were ready for it, to care for others physically or financially and put their needs before your own. You are a hero for boxing up your dreams and putting them in the attic for a little while, but I know the question of "what's next" is still important to you.

Regardless of where you are, I don't think it's too much of a stretch to assume that if you're reading this book, you're probably having a hard time finding an answer to the question "What's next?" And if that's the case, you just read a whole bunch of examples that illustrate a comforting fact: you're not alone. But the comfort of not being alone isn't good enough, is it? You're not heartless, but really, who cares if other people are having a hard time discovering what's next for them? How does that *help* you? You want to know what you're supposed to do.

Well, here's the good news: The rest of this book is designed to help you figure that out. And the first step is to consider what you are really looking for.

WHAT WE'RE LOOKING FOR

After working and talking with so many people in transition (and being there myself)—after hearing their stories, their dreams, and their problems—I've gradually come to the conclusion that we all have something in common. Although our reasons for asking "what's next" may differ, all of us want to find purpose and fulfillment in what we do, including our jobs. See if you agree with me . . .

First, we want to feel a sense of *purpose*—to have a reason for doing whatever it is we are doing. We want a good answer to the question "Why am I doing this?" Very simply, we want to know that we are doing something meaningful. Whether we're in a high-power job that makes us rich or doing repetitive tasks that bore us, we want to know that our contribution matters to the big picture. All of us long to know that there's a reason behind our existence—that our lives are in some way important.

Is this true for you? Do you want your life to mean something? On a scale from 1 to 10, from pointless to meaningful, how do you rate the sense of purpose you have in your current or most recent job? What would you like that number to be?

I have a theory about why a sense of purpose is so important to us: This world is a big place, and we share it with a lot of people. When I fly over a city at night—in the cabin, not the cockpit—I like to look down and think about how each glittering streetlight or house light or car light represents someone's existence. I imagine their stories. In just a few moments, the lives of thousands of people flash by—all those lives, a lot like mine, yet completely different. I'm amazed at the size of the world in which we live. This is a *big* place! And the more technologically advanced we become, the more of the world we get to observe. I think this may have led us to struggle more intensely with our desire to matter. In relation to the whole world, we feel like a tiny speck. We want to know that our lives mean something, that our existence in the world is part of a bigger plan and that we are accomplishing something great. We want to know we are special and important to our families and friends. We want to know that in our jobs—jobs that take up a large portion of our waking hours—we are not just pawns in the grand scheme of a massive world economy. We want to believe that the tasks to which we dedicate our lives make a difference in the world, or at least in the life of someone we know and care about.

We long to matter and to make a difference, and these desires shape the search for what's next. Although we may not go so far as to say we don't care about how much money we make, we want a sense of confidence that our everyday tasks affect the world in a positive way.

Second, we want some level of *fulfillment*—the sense of satisfaction we have when we've done a job well. We feel fulfilled when we enjoy what we do, do it successfully, and are appreciated for doing it. I don't think I've ever talked to anyone who doesn't want to enjoy his or her work and achieve some level of accomplishment.

As I've talked with members of my staff, I've heard many different definitions of what it means to enjoy work. Some want to experience adventure and travel the world, while others want to care for children, create or capture beauty, or compete at the highest levels of a sport.

What would enjoying a job look like for you? What would give you a sense of satisfaction or accomplishment?

Accomplishment, like enjoyment, looks different for different people. Some people are all about the cash and want to reach a high level of wealth. Others couldn't care less about money and would find fulfillment in knowing they are helping people.

This isn't about how important the job seems to be. I immediately think of the team of people working in the restaurant I manage. A few of these individuals take a lot of pride in their jobs. A salad is not a salad unless the customer they hand it to smiles at how beautiful it looks and how good it tastes. A milkshake is not a milkshake unless a child giggles at the whipped topping with gummy worms sticking out of it. These individuals may still be asking what's next, but in the meantime, they've found a way to find purpose and fulfillment in their current jobs.

What about you? Do you want to find purpose and fulfillment in your work and in your life? Do you want to enjoy going to work while also knowing that you are accomplishing something great? I think for most of us, the answer to those questions is obviously yes! Throughout the rest of this book I will present some ideas for how you might discover purpose and fulfillment while also discovering an answer to the question "What's next?" My prayer is that you will ultimately discover hope and freedom. Hope that answers are coming, and freedom from having to figure it out all on your own.

WHAT'S NEXT

1. Which "team" are you on? If you didn't identify with one of the teams described above, write a paragraph describing your "team." Specifically, what has brought you to this point of asking "What's next?"

2. What does a job have to provide in order for you to feel a sense of purpose and fulfillment?

2

THE ELUSIVE DREAM JOB

Let's face it: we know lots of people who have gone their whole lives without ever finding a dream job that brings them happiness or fulfillment. Some of them knew specifically what they wanted to do but never found the means to accomplish it. Others were dissatisfied but could never figure out what they'd rather do. They just grudgingly bore the work with an eye to retirement, or they hopped from job to job always hoping the next thing would be "it."

When my dream of becoming a pilot didn't work out, I started looking for another adventurous occupation. At one point, I considered following in my uncle's footsteps and becoming an FBI agent. At the time, all I could think about was how cool it would be to get in gunfights and catch bad guys.

One day, my uncle took me to his office so I could see what

it was like to save the world as a crime-fighter. He is understandably proud of his job with the FBI, and it excited him that someone else in the family showed interest. I was excited too! I couldn't wait to wear a bulletproof vest while interviewing incarcerated informants. As I rode in the passenger seat of my uncle's black sedan, I wondered who we might interrogate first. *Cue dream sequence.* I began to think of what questions my uncle may need *me* to ask. Maybe I would be the good cop, and he would be the bad cop—sorry, *agent.* Or maybe the roles would be reversed. I began to imagine how epic it would feel to slam a bad guy's forehead into the desk to get him to talk. I hoped I was strong enough to knock the truth out of him.

When we drove up to my uncle's office—*end dream sequence*—I was surprised to find that it looked like . . . well, like an office. At the front door, my uncle didn't push secret numbers into a keypad releasing a hand scanner or voice-recognition microphone. He just used a normal key. It got worse. We walked inside, and he had an oak desk, a blocky white computer, white paper, and black pens. No interrogation rooms with one-way-mirrors, gray lamps, and metal tables. Instead, there was a conference room with a wooden table, executive chairs, and the spaceship-looking thingy that helped with conference calls. I was even more surprised to discover that my uncle did a lot of his investigations from his desk with just his phone and his computer. What? No red phone to call the Oval Office? No secret lever on the bookshelf to open up a wall revealing a hidden gunroom filled with exotic weapons?

I lost interest in the FBI that day. I didn't want to do office work; I wanted to live on the edge.

Was my dream wrong? Did I need to compromise? What could provide what I was looking for?

FRUSTRATED

When we're asking what's next, it can be hard to find answers. As a result, many of us are frustrated. But I think our frustration goes deeper than simply not knowing what's next. Many of us are frustrated because we can't land the dream job our culture tells us we should pursue.

If you Google "dream job" you'll get nearly one *billion* results. Everyone offers 10 tips or 4 steps or promises results in 30 days or by the end of the year—even if you're unqualified—and, oh, good news, if you don't know what your dream job is yet, there are over a million quizzes to help you figure it out. The message is that you should find excitement in your career. You should love your job so much that it doesn't even feel like a job. And the promise is that if you just try hard enough you can accomplish anything!

This all sounds great, but is it true? Should we follow the 7 steps, 5 steps, or 4 steps? Are they guaranteed to work? Do they work half of the time? Do they work for a small group of people some of the time? Do they ever work? These are important questions to consider before you or I buy into the idea that a dream job is just a hop, skip, and a jump in the direction of wanting it bad enough.

Many of the people I work with are searching for the career of their dreams. Some are just trying to make ends meet, but others want so much more than a paycheck. Unfortunately, many of them—like me—have struggled to find the dream career that they thought was promised to anyone who wants it bad enough. They've heard the promises and taken the quizzes, but they have yet to see results.

Meet Ryan: If you walk into the restaurant where I work,

you might find Ryan flipping burgers, scooping ice cream, or counting inventory. But his restaurant skills are only one part of his story.

Ryan has been fishing for over twenty years. His dad taught him on a local lake, and Ryan's first fishing memory is of dropping a baby catfish on his foot. The barb of the catfish was pointing straight down when the fish fell off the hook and landed on his toe. His toe bled but he didn't cry (at least that's the story he tells).

In college, Ryan took a short break from fishing and played Division I football. After two years, however, he decided to transfer to a community college and pursue a degree in the field of his dreams—Fish and Wildlife. With his competitive nature, Ryan decided to pursue professional fishing. He was getting a lot better at catching monster bass, and fishing was—and is—a growing sport. He knew could catch fish like they do in the major tournaments because he was already catching them for fun. Ryan went on to qualify for and compete in three FLW College National Championship Fishing Tournaments and two BassMaster Collegiate Series Tournaments. He was on his way. An exciting, competitive career? Check. Something he loved so much that it wouldn't even feel like a job? Check. A career that matched his skills and qualifications? Check and check.

So why is Ryan still working at a burger restaurant?

I'll let Ryan answer for himself: "When you watch these professional tournaments—or any professional sport—you think talent is a hundred percent of the reason those guys are on TV. Not only that, but many of the interviews with professional athletes are filled with phrases like, 'if you try hard enough you can make it.' What they don't tell you is how much money it takes to enter the big tournaments. I know so many amazing fishermen who can go to just about any lake and bring up monster fish but who would also never have the ability to risk a bunch of money on a tournament. It would take their whole life savings to get in, and what if they have a bad day? Pursuing a dream like fishing is not as easy as it seems, and it's not just a matter of who has the talent."

Ryan—who has already competed at a much higher level than most fishermen—has struggled to break into the big leagues of fishing. And this isn't the only wall he's hit in pursuing a dream career in wildlife. When a few coveted game warden positions opened up, he had the correct college degree to qualify and should have had a great chance at one of the open positions. Yes, "should have"—he didn't get the job.

Ryan is not the only person I know who was qualified for a position in his or her career field of choice but was passed over for someone else. Not the only one whose dream is just out of reach. His story illustrates something that is true for so many.

And yet, movies, talk shows, professional leagues, books, and universities have promised you that dream jobs exist for anyone who tries hard enough. With our culture's can-do attitude, it's easy for the voices in your head to turn on you. *What's wrong with me? I must not be trying hard enough. My dreams feel impractical. I really have no idea what I want to do. I feel stuck.*

It can be so tempting to give up. When you hear of all those other people who seem to have accomplished what you can't, instead of feeling encouraged that the dream is possible, you just feel defeated.

CLOSE ENOUGH TO TASTE IT

Some people really do get there—some people know what they want and find a job they love. But even for them, the journey is sometimes overwhelming and ugly. And sometimes they live that life for a while—and then things fall apart.

When we were in college, I walked into my friend's dorm room one day to find him reading a book on stocks. When I asked Ben what class it was for, he told me: "It's not for a class, I just like researching how the markets work." *Really?* I thought. *Who does that?* Ben does. He dreamed of building wealth for others and for himself by researching the stock market and managing portfolios.

Ben clearly knew what his dream job was. After college, he worked several different jobs. He did everything he could to make his dream of becoming a financial planner a reality, but several years went by as he searched for his opportunity. Finally, a promising spot with a premier company opened up; Ben applied and was accepted. Everything was great!

He had accomplished his goal, and it was even better than he had imagined. I remember calling him one time, and he told me he couldn't talk because he was at the beach with his wife for a training seminar. I think they were staying at a Hilton—right on the water—and all of their meals were paid for. Living the dream.

A few months later, however, Ben called to let me know that his portfolio had fallen one account shy of making the cut, and he had been fired from his dream job.

Here was a guy who got close to exactly what he wanted, and then his dream job slipped away. What happened? Did he fall out of favor with God? Had he done something wrong?

Eventually Ben ended up with another company and he is currently thriving as a financial planner. But even in the good news of him making it, there's a caution for those of us who are looking for the career of our dreams. Although Ben loves his job, it isn't quite as dreamy as he expected. You know why? Because it's a lot harder than he expected! I think that might be the case with most dream jobs; they end up being, well, jobs. Jobs that require hard work.

So what if we never find a dream job? Or what if our dream job ends up being far less dreamy than we imagine? These are important questions because many of us are putting a whole lot of effort into this pursuit.

Spoiler alert: As we work through the rest of this book, I hope you will find that life is so much more than what you do for a living. Here's why: many of us can think of someone who gives pedicures, collects trash, or shines shoes, and who also seems to be one of the happiest people we've ever met. My fisherman friend Ryan, for example. He is an inspiring guy who has not once given in to self-pity. He comes to work every day with an incredible work ethic and attitude. How can that be? Is flipping burgers really the dream job this guy pictured as a ten-year-old dreamer? Is trimming and polishing other people's toenails really the ideal career for the woman we ask for by name at the local salon? Or have they found something much more important to live for—something bigger than a dream job—that allows them to approach every day with contagious joy and inspiring passion?

WHAT'S NEXT

1. What's the story of your dream job journey? If you don't have even a glimmer of an idea of what your dream job would be, why do you think that is?

2. What if you never find a dream job? Could you still enjoy your life? What would that look like?

3

THE CALL OF GOD

For Christians, the search for what's next and the frustration over not landing the dream job can be even more confusing than for those outside the faith. Like everyone else, we want a purposeful and fulfilling occupation. Like everyone else, we want a job that we will truly enjoy, that won't feel like drudgery. But we also long for something even deeper: we desire to discover God's will for our lives. We believe that He *should* have something to say about our futures because, well, He's God and He made each of us. We think this means the choice of a job is not fully up to us. It's a little like a healthy marriage, this becoming a Christian thing. Decisions now require the agreement of two parties instead of just one.

We can add this group to our team roster: Team Called. If you're on Team Called, you expect God to tell you what to do. This was my team. In our desire to please God, we usually want to wait until He tells us what to do—especially when making those really big decisions in life, like searching for the right spouse, the right career path, the right ministry. We don't want to get those big things wrong. If you're on Team Called, you might still be on one of those other teams that we mentioned in chapter 1, but you're asking, "What's next, *God*?" And in the transition time, you're waiting for Him to answer.

In the Christian context, this moment of hearing from God is usually referred to as "the call of God." I don't know about you, but I grew up hearing *a lot* about that subject.

During my senior year of high school, I was struggling to figure out what I should do with my life. I had already given up on the Air Force Academy and was in the process of choosing a college. I applied to a state school that I really wanted to attend, especially because many of my friends were going there. Unfortunately, all of my desire to attend this university couldn't make up for my less-than-stellar effort in high school. (I fell asleep in class a lot and hardly ever studied.) As you can imagine, my lack of effort led to less-than-stellar grades, which led to . . . well, I already told you—I was rejected by the university. All of my friends knew where they were going in August, but I had no idea what to do next.

The idea of God calling me to something special sounded pretty cool, and I was already looking for it, but my search wasn't going anywhere. I had been asking God to reveal His will, but He was being pretty quiet about it. So when I heard about a "calling class" at my church, I signed up immediately.

TRYING TOO HARD

On the first day of the series, I walked into the cold, cafeteria-like room. The floor was made of tile, the walls were painted almost white, and the whole room felt sanitized. Come to think of it, it kind of *smelled* sanitized. I guess it had just been cleaned. The purpose of the gathering was to consider what a calling looks like and to discover if you were one of the special people God had picked—like for a playground dodgeball team. I really wanted to be on the team and, from looking around, I guessed a lot of other people did too. At the end of the series of classes, the pastor was going to lead a ceremony in which he would hand out certificates to all of the "called."

I was excited. In just a few short weeks (or maybe today, on day 1), God would reveal to me His plan for my life. What was He going to say? Where would I be living? What would I be doing? I had no idea what to expect, but I eagerly anticipated some major answers—even if it meant sitting in a cold room for an hour or so each week.

During this class, several church leaders taught that God had a special assignment for my life—something I was uniquely equipped to handle and specifically gifted to complete. They said this assignment was God's calling on my life, and I needed to discover this calling in order to experience true fulfillment and purpose. (Do those words sound familiar?)

The class emphasized being "called" to the mission field, "called" into ministry, or "called" to serve in the church. The speakers made such a big deal out of the people who were called to ministry that it sounded as if the people called to ministry were somehow closer to God and more special to Him than everyone else. As a result of their teaching, I concluded that my church consisted of two groups—the called (the A-team) and the uncalled (the B-team), and God especially favored the A-team.

Consider it my human pride or my immature faith, but I wanted to be on the A-team—I wanted to be one of the called.

I mean, who wants to be on the B-team and ride the bench or be a water boy? Am I right? As a result, I got to the end of the class and made it known to the leadership team that I was one of those people God spoke to—someone God *needed* in the starting lineup to do His real ministry here on earth. They celebrated with me, and I was presented with my official certificate. (I think I still have it stored away somewhere.)

The problem is, I didn't receive a specific calling during the class. I kind of lied about that. But in my mind, it was okay to tell this little fib because I was convinced that my specific calling was on its way. I believed that when God was ready for me to find out what it was, He would let me know. I just needed to be faithful and keep searching.

Unfortunately, God continued to stay rather silent on this subject long after the class ended. I would pray and seek, and seek and pray, and God would sit back and listen—*only* listen. In contrast to what the class had taught, and as far as I could tell, God had no interest in telling me His plan for my life. The pursuit of God's calling felt like a high-stakes game of holy hide-and-seek, and the entire world was the playground. God had hid my calling well—too well!

> THE PURSUIT OF GOD'S CALLING
> FELT LIKE A HIGH-STAKES GAME
> OF HOLY HIDE-AND-SEEK,
> AND THE ENTIRE WORLD
> WAS THE PLAYGROUND.

For a long time, I thought that meant I wasn't holy enough or listening well enough. I thought I had missed something.

Over the years, however, I've met a lot of other people who haven't discovered their callings either, many of them stuck in transition.

Why wouldn't—doesn't—God answer? Many of us believe we need to discover His calling in order to be obedient to Him and please Him with our lives. Why won't God tell us which college to go to, or what to major in, or which career field to choose? Why doesn't He direct us to a more meaningful job, the one we would feel passionate about and love to jump out of bed for each day?

MAKING ASSUMPTIONS

Looking back, I can now see that my expectations of how God should speak to me were based on two assumptions. First, I assumed God wanted me to find a job that gave me purpose and fulfillment. Seems like a safe assumption, right? Doesn't it make sense that God would want me to experience enjoyment and accomplishment in my work?

Second, I was keenly aware of how much time is dedicated to a job, and I also knew my life needed to be dedicated to God. As a result, I grew up assuming God's call would be directly related to what I did for a living (my dream job). Again, it only makes sense. Why would God have me spend forty-five hours a week doing something unrelated to His will or calling? I didn't think He would.

My two assumptions—that God wanted me to enjoy my work and that my job and calling would be related—led me to combine my desire for a dream job with my pursuit of God's call. In other words, I had expected that my dream job and my calling would be the same thing.

Where did I get that idea?

It started in the calling class, but it didn't end there. There are many Christian speakers, bloggers, and leaders who urge us to pursue our dreams, because that's what God wants for us . . . what He's *called* us to do . . . the very purpose for which He made us. We can become so desperate to discover God's call for our lives that we buy whatever promises us the answers. I have a whole shelf of books on the subjects of dream jobs and callings. I have numerous podcasts and links to several blogs on these subjects. Even seminaries promote this idea. Although I really enjoyed seminary and learned a lot there, the most frustrating class for me was a required seminar describing God's calling as a dream-like job. According to the professor, God is eagerly waiting to tell us what to do, and we just need to listen close enough and seek His will to figure it out. If we do, we will discover the perfect fit—the intersection of God's will and the purpose and fulfillment for which we long. Seminaries have long blurred the lines between a dream job and the call of God, and that idea has now permeated our thinking so that we've never paused to say, *Really? Where is that in the Bible?*

Here's the thing: I believe God created you in His image and likeness and sees you as His kid. I believe God loves you so much, and that He wants you to find purpose and fulfillment in your life. I think God is "calling" out to you to offer hope if you feel stuck, and to set you free from the anxiety of what's next so you can thrive in your life and career.

But I don't think "dream job" and "God's call" are the same thing.

So that's what I want to spend the rest of this book examining. I want to look at what the idea of "calling" looks like in the Bible. Who were some of the people called by God, and what did that look like for them? What does that word *calling* even mean? Maybe through examining these stories, we will see what it looks like when God shows up and says, "Hey you! I want you to do this."

WHAT'S NEXT

1. What do you believe about the call of God? Where did that belief originate? If you've ever perceived that God called you to do something, describe that experience.

2. Think of a Christian who works in a "secular" job—not in a ministry or other Christian setting—and who reflects the love and grace of Jesus on the job. Whose name comes to mind? What is it about him or her that stands out to you?

4

A GUY
NAMED MOSES

Even people who have never read the Bible before have probably heard of Moses. He's kind of a big deal in the religious traditions of Judaism, Islam, and Christianity. But who was he, really? And what did his calling from God look like?

Moses was born at a time when the Hebrews were slaves to the Egyptians, and the ruling pharaoh had ordered all of the Hebrew boy babies to be killed. With some stealth and ingenuity, Moses's family kept him alive long enough to—long story short—be rescued by Pharaoh's own daughter. (How's that for irony?) As a result, Moses grew up in the palace as the foster child of Pharaoh.

Even though he was a prince of Egypt, like many foster kids Moses had the desire to be connected to his true heritage. One day he saw an Egyptian beating up a Hebrew slave, so he murdered the Egyptian and buried him in the sand before anyone could see. Like in a modern movie where the perpetrator didn't cover his tracks as well as he thought he did, someone noticed Moses's actions and reported the murder to Pharaoh, who then tried to kill Moses. Moses fled, married a woman in another country, and—in transition—became a shepherd.

IN TRANSITION

> Moses was keeping the flock of his father-in-law Jethro, the priest of Midian; he led his flock beyond the wilderness, and came to Horeb, the mountain of God. There the angel of the LORD appeared to him in a flame of fire out of a bush. (Exodus 3:1–2)

Notice the contrast between Moses's first life in the palace and his new life as a shepherd. Instead of a palace, Moses is in the wilderness. Instead of being tended to by servants, Moses is tending someone else's sheep. Already, many of us can relate to Moses (except for the whole former-royalty thing). Here's a guy who had everything and lost it. Life fell apart.

Have you ever been in a similar situation? Maybe you had a long-term relationship with someone you were 100 percent sure was "the one," but it ended. Or maybe you lost your job and are now—like Moses—working a dead-end job at minimum wage. Or maybe you were going to take over the family business, and then the business was sold or went bankrupt. Or maybe . . . or maybe . . . or maybe. Many of us have seen a good life seemingly fall apart—maybe our own. Some of us doubt we've ever experienced the good life in the first place.

It sounds to me like Moses's life is not all bad, though. He's now married and has a job, even if it's not a job he's proud of.

At that time, being a shepherd had about as much prestige as pumping sewage out of a port-a-jon after a professional sporting event. It was a dirty job, and society looked down on shepherds.

Not only was Moses tending someone else's sheep, but Moses was also deep in the wilderness. But he didn't stop there. Look at the verse again; Moses pushed the sheep "beyond" the wilderness. The word literally means "after"—What comes after the wilderness? Maybe he needed to get away for a while and clear his head. Maybe he was hoping he'd get lost and be unable to find his way back to his—what some would consider—pathetic life.

And then God shows up, beyond the wilderness.

Think about that for a moment.

Moses is walking in some sort of countryside beyond the wilderness when suddenly a thorn bush (the Hebrew word means "briar") starts burning but doesn't burn up. It's like a briar-shaped butane lighter without the butane. Naturally, Moses is curious and wants to check it out. If that's not weird enough, the flame-broiled briar starts to speak. Okay, not the bush exactly, but God, who has taken up residence in the bush: "I am the God of your father, the God of Abram, the God of Isaac, and the God of Jacob" (3:6). In other words, "I'm your God, Moses, the God of your family. The God who has been taking care of you and your ancestors for generations." God continues: "I have observed the misery of my people who are in Egypt; I have heard their cry on account of their taskmasters. Indeed, I know their sufferings, and I have come down to deliver them from the Egyptians, and to bring them up out of that land to a good and broad land, a land flowing with milk and honey" (3:7–8).

Look at how personal God is and how active He is in caring

for His kids: He has *observed* their misery . . . *heard* their cry . . . He *knows* their sufferings . . . He has *come* down to *deliver* them and *bring* them out. This is really good news for Moses, for the Israelites, and for us! Here is the God who observes, hears, knows, and delivers those who are in misery—who feel all hope is lost. If you're in a tough situation, this is really good news for you too. God hears and delivers. God is coming. You are not alone.

EXCUSE ME?

I think you can imagine how excited Moses would have been. Finally, God was coming to deliver the Israelites from slavery. Wahoo!

But then God pulls maybe the first historical example of a bait and switch, and Moses and God end up in a debate. God tells Moses, "So come, I will send you to Pharaoh to bring my people, the Israelites, out of Egypt" (3:10). Listen to Moses's understandable response in verse 11: "Say what? I thought you said *you* were coming to deliver them!" (author's paraphrase).

Remember, Moses ran away from Egypt because Pharaoh wanted to *kill* him—Moses had a price on his head—and now God wants Moses to go back? And do what? Turn himself in? Actually, no. God wants him to do something even more audacious. God wants him to go to Pharaoh and demand that Pharaoh release all of the slaves—those slaves who have helped build the Egyptian empire. Ha! Right! If Moses were alive today, this would have been the moment when he pulled out some sarcasm: "Sure, God. That will be a very popular idea with Pharaoh!" Unsurprisingly, Moses doesn't accept God's "calling" on his life but instead begins to debate with God.

We can almost tap our feet to the rhythm of the counterpoint: But Moses said (3:11) . . . But God said (3:12) . . . But Moses said (3:13) . . . But God said (3:14) . . .

Can you imagine arguing with God? Some of us can. Some of us have been in tough situations and have argued with God about His timing or what He's allowed to happen in our lives. Another freeing aspect of Moses's story is that our God is big enough, kind enough, and gracious enough to let us ask questions and push back on things we don't like.

What was it that Moses didn't like? He didn't want to do what God was calling him to do. Check out his excuses—excuses to which we can relate:

1. *I'm not prepared for this.* To paraphrase Exodus 3:11, Moses says, "I'm a nobody shepherd in the wilderness. Who am I that I should go before a king and lead a nation of people out of slavery?" Have you ever felt like a nobody? Moses did too. Have you ever felt inadequate? Moses did too. He didn't want to do what God wanted him to do because he felt like he had nothing to offer. Today's version might be, "I work in a restaurant, and you want me to do *that* job, God?" As humans, we struggle with feelings of inadequacy.

2. *I don't know what to say.* Moses's second excuse was that he wouldn't know what to say (3:13). I know what that's like. What can we say when someone's mom dies? What can we say when someone is diagnosed with a terminal disease? What can we say when a family loses their home or business? What words are helpful when life is falling apart for someone we love? Yet these are very real circumstances to which God will call us out of our comfort zone to help and encourage people who

are hurting. I think that the same God who promised to give Moses the words will give you and me the words too.

3. *No one will take me seriously.* Moses's third excuse (4:1) is also super-relatable: What if they don't believe me or listen to what I have to say? Think about the times when you have felt God leading you to pray out loud in a group or to get up and share something great that God has done in your life. Times you've been asked to help someone with a task, teach a workshop, or lead a group. Those situations can be intimidating. We, like Moses, may also want to look at God and say, "Nope! No thank you. I don't think that's a good idea because I wouldn't know what to say. And even if I did know what to say, they probably won't listen to me anyway."

4. *I'm no good at that.* Finally, we come to Moses's last excuse, and this one should be very surprising to those of us who've ever heard someone say, "God's calling on your life will utilize your gifts." Moses looks at God and declares, "You're asking me to do something I'm not good at! I'm not eloquent or a good speaker! I have yet to win any debate contests or be recognized as a rhetorician. In fact, I'm known more for my *inability* to pull phrases together. I used to get bullied for stuttering. All of my witty comments come long after the conversation in which they were needed is over. I can't go speak to a king because I'm not good at speaking" (author's extended paraphrase of Exodus 4:10). How does God respond to Moses? By reminding him that He is the giver of all good gifts like speech. "Then the LORD said to him, 'Who gives speech to mortals? Who makes them mute or deaf, seeing or blind? Is it not I, the LORD? Now go, and I will be with your mouth and teach you what you are to speak'" (4:11–12).

Wow! God doesn't let Moses's ability or inability get in the way. It makes me think God values obedience far above skill. This is good news for us too! When God calls us to do something, He will also help us do it. If you feel God leading you to speak up about something bad that happened—maybe some abuse has occurred or you've seen someone treated unfairly—God will give you the words to say or the strength to do whatever you need to do. Or maybe you feel God asking you to do something outside of your expertise or skill set—don't let your inability, fear, or timidity limit what God can do through you. The God who is prompting you is the same God who gives the right words and the right actions in the right moments.

After considering all of these excuses, Moses's last plea to God makes sense—"O my Lord, please send someone else" (4:13). Unfortunately, at least in Moses's eyes, God continually reassures Moses of something that all of us need to hear too: I will be with you (3:12). Did you catch that? We serve a God who goes with us into every difficult situation, circumstance, or conversation. God doesn't just ask us to do something and then put his feet up while watching TV. God goes with us, guides us, and helps us.

But what does all of this have to do with God's calling? Let's recap. God has specifically asked (called, we might say) Moses to do something. Moses comes up with a bunch of reasons why God's calling makes no sense because he is clearly unqualified for the task. He finally asks God outright to send someone else. It is this final comment that really breaks down the idea that God's calling is going to be to a dream job. I think we can all agree that this call was *not* Moses's dream job. God called Moses to do something he obviously didn't *want* to do. Yet we are often taught through Christian speakers and writers that the God who *called* Moses is the same God who now *calls* us to discover the job of our dreams, our perfect purpose, the thing we were made to do that pulls together all of our gifts and abilities, through which God will shower blessing on us, in which we will find ultimate fulfillment.

I think we need to be careful here.

WHAT'S NEXT

1. Which of Moses's excuses can you relate to? When have you used excuses to get out of something you didn't want to do? What might have happened if you did what you didn't want to do?

2. Read Exodus 3:1–4:17. What does Moses's calling from God communicate about what a calling looks like?

5

A GUY NAMED JONAH

Jonah was a prophet like Moses.

What is a prophet? You know how in the Lord of the Rings trilogy Gandalf the White seemed to always know what was best and what to do? A prophet is kind of like Gandalf. Instead of having intuition and a magic staff, however, God gave the Old Testament prophets a message of truth and some miraculous signs to prove that He had spoken to them. In the story of Moses, for instance, God helped Moses know what to say to Pharaoh, and then gave him a staff that could turn into a snake and back into a staff.

Oftentimes, we think of a prophet's message as a prediction of future events, but that's not always the case. Many prophets were called to proclaim something like, "Hey y'all! You aren't following God's path to human life and flourishing. Instead, you are pursuing things that are going to lead to death and destruction for you and others. God told me to let you know you're destroying yourselves, and that he's holding back all the bad things that should have already happened to you so you have time to change your ways."

Sometimes the people responded to the prophet by stopping bad behavior and following God again. Sometimes they didn't.

There are a lot of similarities between God's call of Moses and God's call of Jonah.

1. Neither prophet wanted to do what God wanted him to do; they didn't recognize God's call as their dream job.

2. Both prophets went to great lengths to try to change God's mind on who He chose to accomplish His will.

3. Both prophets failed to change God's mind and ended up doing what God wanted them to do—it was as if they didn't have a choice.

Unlike Moses, however, Jonah did not get into a debate with God and offer a series of seemingly legitimate excuses. Instead, Jonah tried to skip town.

To understand Jonah's story we have to first consider some context. First, thousands of years ago, and many years before Jonah was born, Israel was a mighty and unified nation. After a civil war, however, the nation split into two separate kingdoms—North and South.

Jonah was a prophet in the Northern Kingdom during a really scary time. The king of the north, Jeroboam II, wanted nothing to do with God or God's ways. He was actively following false gods and leading the Northern Israelites further away from the God who loved them and wanted what was best for them. Not only was the Northern Kingdom in trouble because

Jeroboam II was leading them the wrong way spiritually, but the borders of Israel were a mess—literally, they were mostly torn down by enemy raids, and the army was so small it could hardly defend against attacks. I can't imagine how scary it would have been to live in the Northern Kingdom; probably a lot like living in modern Sudan. Every night, the Israelites went to bed knowing there was an enemy who hated them and there was no defense to keep that enemy away.

Enter Jonah. According to 2 Kings 14, Jonah showed up and gave the people really good news. Although they wanted nothing to do with God—they were actively worshipping other gods—He was still going to protect them by restoring their borders. Here's an interesting factoid for you (just in case you end up on *Jeopardy* one day): guess who God used to restore the borders? Jeroboam II, the king who wanted nothing to do with Him. How's that for a picture of God showing undeserved grace and mercy? "Hey! You want nothing to do with me, but I'm still going to protect you and help you!"

Although the restoration of the borders was a big deal, the Northern Kingdom of Israel was still a complete mess. They needed a prophet to help them understand God's truth and love. They needed a prophet to show them how to follow God again. They needed a Gandalf the White to lead the Fellowship to Mount Doom and help destroy the ring, which in the case of Jeroboam II looked more like pagan idols shaped like cows. Jonah was this Gandalf, their prophet. After the restoration of the walls, there was still so much good Jonah could do in Israel. Let's pick up the story there . . .

The story of Jonah begins exactly how we would expect, "Now the word of the LORD came to Jonah son of Amittai, saying . . ." (Jonah 1:1) Just like He did with other prophets, God showed up to give Jonah a message.

Now you might guess that God went on to say something like, "Go to Israel, help them build up their army so they can protect themselves and show them what it means to follow me. Lead them, Jonah! They need you." Nope! That's not even close to how the story goes. God tells Jonah, "Go at once to Nineveh, that great city, and cry out against it; for their wickedness has come up before me" (v. 2).

Wait! Nineveh? Where's that? Nineveh was not a city in Israel. It was a city in Assyria—a nation that wanted to destroy Israel. They were Israel's archenemies. Yet God called Jonah away from his people, to minister to Israel's enemies. Wait (again)! What? Israel is in trouble! Israel needs help! Jonah speaks Hebrew! Why would God call him to leave?

FATHER KNOWS BEST

I'm reminded of all the times I think I know what's best, and yet God allows things to happen that I don't understand. Sometimes, what happens is the exact opposite of what I think is best. A friend of mine recently applied for a job because the job description was everything he had ever wanted out of a career. He, and I, thought for sure God had finally answered our prayers for him to find the dream job for which God had created him. He didn't get the job, however, and we have had many discussions trying to make sense of his rejection email. Maybe the first lesson of the story of Jonah is that you and I can trust God, even when it doesn't seem to make sense. After all, this story ends up being really good news for the Ninevites. But that's getting ahead of ourselves. Back to Jonah.

God's call away from Israel didn't make any sense to Jonah either. But Jonah's a professional prophet, right? He's a professional pastor who speaks with God regularly and communicates God's wisdom to the masses. In the past, when God asked Jonah to do something (proclaim the good news to Israel about restoring the borders), he did it. Yet the story of Jonah surprises us again . . .

"But Jonah set out to flee to Tarshish from the presence of the LORD" (v. 3). Remember how Moses got into an argument with God and ultimately asked God, "please send someone else"? Maybe Jonah knew how that story ended because he doesn't waste any time in an argument with God. As far as we know, he could have even lied to God and said, "Sure! I'll be glad to go" while secretly looking up discount travel sites on his smartscroll. Instead of going to Nineveh, Jonah gets on a boat and tries to run away from God. He wanted nothing to do with what God wanted him to do, and he tried to escape God's will for his life.

Stop and think about that for a moment. Can you imagine running away from God?

So what happens next? God uses a series of miraculous events, including a giant storm and a giant fish, to dislodge Jonah from his cruise ship (the sailors throw him overboard) and transport him (a big fish swallows him and swims) to the shore near Nineveh. How's that for an epic narrative? Marvel and DC can't touch God's creativity. Now let's skip ahead to the end.

By chapter 4—after Jonah has finally obeyed God and preached to the Ninevites—we find out why Jonah hated God's calling so much. God showed love and mercy to the Ninevites—Israel's enemies—and Jonah couldn't stand the thought of seeing them rescued. He would rather have died than for God to show them compassion.

> "O LORD! Is not this what I said while I was still in my own country? That is why I fled to Tarshish at the beginning; for I knew that you are a gracious God and merciful, slow to anger, and abounding in steadfast love, and ready to relent from punishing. And now, O LORD, please take my life from me, for it is better for me to die than to live." (4:2–3)

Jonah knew why God had called him to go to Nineveh: because God loves all people from all nations, even people from the nations Jonah hated. That's why God didn't let Jonah get out of doing what God wanted him to do; God had a plan to show love and mercy to a bunch of people and He wasn't going to let anything get in the way of accomplishing that mission. And the story of Jonah ends with a somewhat funny final question from God that illustrates His love for people: Shouldn't I care about the great city of Nineveh, in which there are more than a hundred twenty thousand people who don't know the truth, and also lots of cattle (4:11)? Mic drop. The point is, God loves people of all nations—he even loves their animals. God is persistent in showing that love regardless of how a prophet like Jonah responds.

Jonah, like Moses, wanted nothing to do with God's calling on his life. He didn't want to go to Nineveh. He didn't want to tell them the good news that God would show them grace if they asked for it. He didn't want them to repent. He wanted to die rather than obey God. (For a deeper exploration of the story of Jonah, check out the two-week radio series on *Discover the Word* at discovertheword.org.)

GOD CALLING

It's clear that God didn't call Moses and Jonah to their dream jobs. These stories offer a completely different perspective on what God's calling may look like, and I think we need to consider these narratives as we attempt to discover what God is calling us to do.

In Moses's story, we saw that God doesn't always call us into something that utilizes our strengths, but God also doesn't leave us on our own. Over and over again, God said He would go with Moses and help him accomplish all God had called him to accomplish. I think God helps us too. You and I can step into the calling of God because, just like in the story of Moses, God is with us and will help us.

In Jonah's story, not only was Jonah *not* called to a dream job but God asked Jonah to do something Jonah didn't understand. The call didn't make sense. By the end of the story, however, God's calling on Jonah's life makes perfect sense: God loves all people from all nations, and nothing—including a stubborn prophet—can get in the way of God's love. I think this applies to us too. God's calling represents His heart and mission for the world. Jonah was asked to represent the heart of God by reaching out to a people group unlike his own to proclaim God's love and mercy. God has a big heart and a moving mission, and when He calls us to participate it will be to help promote His messages of hope, freedom, and love to a broken world.

These stories are not exhaustive of the ways God calls people in Scripture (we will look at a few more examples in chapter 15), and I'm not suggesting that they should be prescriptive for the way we expect God to call all people. But these biblical examples must at least inform the way we approach the call of God as we understand the stories within the context of who God is—a good father who loves us.

WHAT'S NEXT

1. Have you ever tried to hide from God or to run away from Him? Did it work? What brought you back to Him?

2. Read Jonah 1–4. What does Jonah's story communicate about the heart and purposes of God?

6

A LOOK AT
FATHER GOD

It was raining.

Of course it was raining. Sara lived in Oregon, near the coast, and it was always raining—at least that's how she felt. Lately, however, the daily drizzle that was once so annoying seemed to suit the state of her emotions. She was a senior in high school and just weeks away from graduation. Two different universities had already accepted her, but she couldn't decide which one to attend. The schools were nothing alike, which meant it was nearly impossible for her to consider the pros and cons of each. If they had been similar, she could have analyzed each school and made a decision to attend whichever stood out as the better option. But they weren't the same at all.

Sara's first option—the college her dad wanted her to attend—was known for its law program. Sara didn't really want to study law, but her dad was insistent. He wanted her to be successful and to follow in the family business. Nearly every person in Sara's family had become a lawyer and had attended that particular college. It was a good school—a top-tier university, in fact—and Sara's dad told her over and over again how thankful she should be for the opportunity to attend a college most people only wished they could attend (and that he was willing to pay for).

Sara's second option—the one she was passionately excited about—was to study photography and graphic design at a local technical college. She had always loved photography and design. In the past few years, she had spent her summers traveling around Oregon, capturing the diverse beauty of various landscapes. It made her feel alive to capture Oregon's uniqueness through the lens of a camera. Her favorite photos—the ones she was most proud of—were close-up shots of the moss-covered trees in a nearby national forest.

Sara tried to explain her struggle to her father many times. "Dad, I want to make you happy. I want to please you and please the family. But I don't think I'm cut out to be a lawyer."

"What do you mean 'not cut out to be a lawyer'?" her dad retorted. "You have excellent grades. You've been accepted into one of the top pre-law programs in the county, your family has studied law for generations, and look at the way you're arguing with me right now! If anyone is 'cut out' to be a lawyer, it's you."

"But I don't really want to study law. I want to take pictures—to capture moments and scenes most people miss. You've seen what I can do. These are good photographs, and if I studied more I could . . . "

"Sara! These photos are pretty, but anyone with a smartphone can capture pictures of trees. That's not a job; it's a cheap hobby that will leave you without a paycheck and sleeping on my couch."

Sara stopped talking and tears filled her eyes. She didn't make another sound but simply left the room. Her dad was also quiet. He knew he had gone too far, but he felt like he needed to make it clear that her aspirations were silly. In his mind, photography just wasn't a viable career option for his daughter.

As you read Sara's story, what did you think about her dad? Is he a good father or a bad father?

The answer to that question is tricky because our interpretation of the story depends on our experiences. I think all of us can agree that her dad's final comment went too far. Even if it could be argued that he was looking at the situation objectively, he went about it the wrong way. He attacked her skill, belittled her ability and passions, and demoralized her.

But there's another side to the story. Sara's dad truly wanted what was best for his daughter, and he knew how difficult it would be for her to build a successful career in an oversaturated market. Ask any photographer who has built a successful business—or one who hasn't. He or she will tell you that it is really, *really* difficult to stand out because there are so many people who claim to be professional photographers. On the other hand, if Sara followed in the footsteps of her dad and the rest of her family, she would have a somewhat guaranteed and well-paying job after college. So even though Sara's dad spoke rudely to her, he really was trying to look out for her the best he knew how.

Was Sara's dad a good father or a bad father? The answer is not quite as simple as we might want to think.

GOOD AND PERFECT

Have you ever heard a version of Sara's story before? Maybe in a movie, where the dad wanted his son to be a doctor, but the son wanted to start a coffee shop instead. I'm not sure who decided that becoming a lawyer or doctor was a bad thing, but at some point a director in Hollywood felt those two occupations were in stark contrast to the dreams of young people. Maybe the director's parents wanted him to become a lawyer, but he wanted to "make movies" instead. I have to admit—the contrast between a dad's desire and a child's desire is a powerful way to express the struggle to find one's place in the world.

Sadly, many Christians see God the Father through a similar lens. We've bought into the stereotypical thinking that tells us that being obedient to God's will means that we'll have to give up what we love. In fact, in chapters 4 and 5 we considered the stories of Moses and Jonah, which—if we're honest—seem to indicate that God could call us and force us to do things we don't want to do. Without the context of all the other stories and teachings of Scripture, the God of Moses's and Jonah's stories seems a lot like Sara's dad. (Notice I said, God could *seem* like Sara's dad. Hold on to that idea for a bit, and we will revisit it later.)

But is this really who God is? Does this really express what God wants for our lives? I don't think so. I think the Bible shows us a different God than the one many of us have been conditioned to expect.

One of the most repeated names for God in the Bible is "Father." The Bible doesn't describe Him as any ol' father, though; He is a *good* Father. Consider the following example:

> Don't bargain with God. Be direct. Ask for what
> you need. This isn't a cat-and-mouse, hide-and-seek

game we're in. If your child asks for bread, do you
trick him with sawdust? If he asks for fish, do you
scare him with a live snake on his plate? As bad as
you are, you wouldn't think of such a thing. You're
at least decent to your own children. *So don't you
think the God who conceived you in love will be even
better?* (Matthew 7:7–11 MSG)

Jesus does something very powerful in this passage. He con-
trasts a human father's desire for what's best for his child with
God the Father's desire for what's best for all His children. Most
of the dads listening to Jesus that day were probably decent
fathers. Like Sara's dad, they wanted what was best for their
sons or daughters. Unfortunately, also like Sara's dad, their
understanding of how to provide for their kids was influenced
by their own brokenness.

In *The Message* quoted above, Eugene Peterson paraphrased
it, "As bad as you are," but the majority of translations call
human fathers "evil" (which is an accurate translation of the
Greek *ponērós*):

If you then, *who are evil*, know how to give good
gifts to your children, how much more will your
Father in heaven give good things to those who ask
him!

Matthew 7:11, 7-Eleven; that makes me want a Slurpee. Okay,
seriously though, I don't know about you, but I'm not a fan
of being called "evil." With that said, however, I do know I
am by no means a perfect dad. I've incorrectly disciplined my
kids. I've misunderstood a situation and put the wrong kid in

timeout. I've had to apologize to my kids for raising my voice. I've been unreasonable, and I've expected more than I should from a nine-, seven-, and five-year-old. I've even given them the good gift of a Slurpee and then stolen back a sip or two.

I think Jesus knew there were dads in His audience who, like me, had made mistakes. I also think He knew that everyone listening to Him that day could think of moments when their own father made a mistake. And then there were probably men and women in the audience who knew exactly what it meant to have an "evil" father. Maybe some of their dads were drunks who neglected them, and maybe others were emotionally or physically abusive.

I'm reminded of a foster-parent training that my wife and I attended. In the class, the social worker—who spends at least fifty hours a week working with broken families—told us that even in the worst situations, he has yet to find a dad that did everything wrong. He knows of dads who have abused their kids, and yet bought them the perfect Christmas present. It happens.

Although even the best human daddies are imperfect, almost all dads—even those broken and "evil" fathers—know better than to give their kids sawdust to eat or dangerous snakes to play with.

And here's the really, *really* good news for all of us. In contrast to human daddies who are imperfect, Jesus proclaims that God—a God who lives in heaven and who is perfect in every way—is a Father who gives even better gifts. If you can think about all of the ways in which your dad fell short, you can know that God the Father doesn't fall short in any of them. If you can think of all the ways in which your dad messed up as a parent, you can be confident that God the Father doesn't mess up in any of those ways. More than that, if you can think of all the good gifts your imperfect daddy gave you, you can be sure that your good and perfect Father in heaven will provide for you in better ways than you could even imagine (see Ephesians 3:20–21). Even though the best human dads get it wrong sometimes, God is the perfect Dad who gets it right 100 percent of the time.

I think a disclaimer is needed here, because I know what some people—ahem, me—might be thinking: What about the times it doesn't feel like God gets it right? What about the times it feels like God the Father has let you or me down? Those are really good and really important questions, to which there are no easy answers. My encouragement would be for you to go to God the Father with those questions. Tell God when you feel He let you down. Ask Him, "Why did you let this happen, God? Where were you when I needed you most?" God is big enough to take it—to take on your difficult questions. He may not answer in the way you want, but I know from experience that even in the darkest situations, God can bring peace where there is no peace. End disclaimer.

DOESN'T PLAY GAMES

Now back to our passage from Matthew. Interestingly—and in a very applicable way to our discussion—the context of these verses is Jesus describing the process of seeking and asking God for help. Did you notice the first line? Jesus said, "Don't bargain with God. Be direct. Ask for what you need."

I'm guessing that the people Jesus talked to that day wanted help from God, and from first glance it seems that Jesus was telling them that they needed only to ask. Evidently, if we need help from God, we need only ask Him for help, and our good Father in heaven will take care of it.

Can I be transparent with you? I haven't always found this promise to be true—at least in the way I've understood it in the past. In chapter 3, I described a high-stakes game of hide-and-seek—God hiding His call for my life while I tried to seek it out. Yet even after months and years of praying for God to reveal His calling and will to me, I still searched for both.

According to Eugene Peterson, God doesn't play "cat-and-mouse" or "hide-and-seek" games. Yet that is exactly the way in which I describe my search for God's calling. So where did I go wrong? What have I missed? If God is a good Father who gives good gifts, why is He withholding the good gift of His will from me—His child?

Renowned Bible scholar Dr. Bruce Waltke puts the question this way:

> If we accept the fact that our heavenly Father loves us, and that we are His children, does it make sense that He would hide His will from us? . . .
>
> When I hear Christians talking about the will of God, they often use phrases such as "If only I could find God's will," as though He is keeping it hidden from them, or "I'm praying that I'll discover His will for my life," because they apparently believe the Lord doesn't want them to find it, or that He wants to make it as hard as possible for them to find so that they will prove their worth.
>
> . . . So does it make sense that He would play some sort of game with His children, hiding His will? Is it logical that the God who says He has a

plan for each life would conceal that plan so that
His work cannot go forward through His people?[1]

Dr. Waltke is suggesting that if we really believe that God is a good Father, we can't also believe He will play games with us or that He would hide His will from those He loves. Those ideas are in contrast to and incompatible with a concept of Father God. If God is a loving Father, He will eagerly share with us what He has planned for our lives.

Regardless of what kind of dad you had, you have some understanding—even if it's not complete—of what a good father looks like. A good father provides for his kids. A good father wants what's best for his children, and he tries to help them get there. A good father is loving and helpful, and he provides direction.

At the same time, I think we can also agree that a good father does not always tell his kids exactly what they should do but sometimes allows them to figure it out on their own. Like a good mentor, a good father asks questions and helps his children figure out what they are supposed to do. Even if the father guides the conversation by asking the right questions and pointing the child in a certain direction, he doesn't always tell his son or daughter, "This is exactly what you should do."

Yet a good father is quick to explain his expectations for how his kids will live their lives, especially in regard to their character and integrity.

My dad spent much of my childhood teaching me expectations. He wanted me to become a man who honored women, served others, worked hard, did well in school, reflected good character, and showed integrity. When I did the opposite of any of these expectations—such as dishonoring my mother—he used discipline to mold and shape my will. My dad was very vocal and clear about what he expected for my life.

Yet every time I asked my dad what job I should take or what career path I should choose, he was slow to help me figure out those things. My dad did not want to tell me what I should do, what I should major in, or whether I should join the family business. Instead, he looked for opportunities to shape and mold my search so I could discover what was in my best interests. He did that without neglecting all of the expectations he had already built into my character. In other words, my dad—a good father—was quick to answer questions about character and slow to answer specific questions about specific jobs.

My mentor was the same way. When I was going through the mentally stressful struggle of trying to figure out what to do with my life, my mentor never told me what he thought I should do. Instead, he asked good questions, gave me a few books to read, and pointed me toward some helpful podcasts. He also spent a lot of time with me. In the same way I have been frustrated with God for not giving me explicit answers, I've been frustrated with my mentor for not helping me choose a specific career path. Yet, looking back, I can now see that both my dad and my mentor were extremely wise *and* good.

What if God is similar to my father and my mentor in the way He deals with questions about His will and what we are supposed to do with our lives?

It makes sense to me that in the same way my dad taught me his expectations of what it means to be a man of character and integrity and to succeed in life, God—who is a far better Father than my earthly dad—has taught me His expectations. My dad—an imperfect father—told me that his will for my life was for me to become a man of integrity and character regardless of my career field.

What if God—a good and perfect Father—is more concerned about our character and shaping us into the men and women He intends for us to become than He is in making sure we do the exact job He would have us do?

WHAT'S NEXT

1. Explain why Sara's dad is a good father or a bad father.

2. Describe a good father. What are his characteristics? What types of things does he do? What wisdom would he share? How would he guide a child into what's best for him or her?

7

A SURPRISING VERSE
ABOUT GOD'S WILL

Have you ever been in a situation where life seemed to fall apart?
Where what you knew to be true was suddenly challenged?
Where everything that was solid under your feet slipped away?

Several years ago now, I was a few weeks away from the
release of my first book, *Ten Days Without*, and had been
invited to speak at an event in Michigan. A lifelong dream (yes,
I've had a few of them)—the dream of publishing a book—
had come true, and I couldn't wait to engage with an audience
around the content I had written.

The Michigan trip would be just the first stop in a month-
long book tour, and I had already set up a few more unpaid
speaking engagements in the Southeast. (When you're a new
author you'll speak anywhere there's a microphone even if they
don't pay you.) Rebecca and I had decided to bring the whole
family and use the time in between gigs as a much-needed
vacation.

Finally, the time came for my first presentation, and my talk went almost exactly as I had expected. Although there were fewer people in the audience than I had hoped, I hit all of the points I wanted to cover. Emotionally I was floating. Getting to speak about the book I had written was even better than I had anticipated.

The moment I was finished, I knew I had nailed it. If there hadn't still been people in the room—or if I had been equipped with a cone of silence—I would have shouted something like *"That. Was. Awesome!"*

A few moments later, after everyone else had left the room, my boss—who was also speaking at the event—congratulated me and told me I had done an excellent job. He told me I communicated each point clearly, and he said the content was going to really help a lot of people. He told me he was proud of me. He told me he was glad he got to see the talk, because he knew I'd be okay.

"Okay"?

And then he fired me.

Freefall.

Like the longest drop of the tallest roller coaster you've ever ridden, except this roller coaster wasn't coming back up. Come to think of it, my heart and stomach felt pretty similar to the way they feel on a roller coaster—hard to breathe on the edge of throwing up.

HELP!

As you might imagine, the next few weeks did not go as expected—for me or for my family. We were hurt; we were angry; and we had no idea what we would do next. A few weeks turned into a month without a job, and my hurt and anger turned into despair. Sure, I could go work at a fast food restaurant, but I didn't want any ol' job—I wanted to find the job God had picked out for me.

So I Googled it. Seriously. I Googled "What is God's will for my life?" If you're smirking right now, that's a good thing— looking back it's almost embarrassing. Anyway, I didn't find most of the links to be helpful. Many of them further blurred and confused the lines between God's calling and the search for a dream job. But after several hours of mind-numbing research, I stumbled across a list of Bible verses related to God's will.

I almost didn't click on the link. Remember chapter 3? I grew up in a church that emphasized searching the Bible for God's call. Yet every time I searched the Bible, no answers appeared. There were times when I thought the Bible offered an answer—like in college, when I thought I should join a children's ministry in South Florida. I remember praying about it and then opening the Bible and pointing haphazardly to a chapter. That chapter happened to be Matthew 19, and I read verse 14: "Let the little children come to me, and do not stop them." Done deal! I'm supposed to have the children come unto me—or was that about Jesus? But I digress.

So when I found a list of verses on "God's will," I was skeptical that they could help me figure out God's calling for my life. I had already tried the Bible route, and it seemed rather quiet on my specific role in God's story for the world. The Scriptures were full of promises about God having a plan but were quiet on the subject of God's plan *for me*.

I clicked on the link and nearly stopped reading after the first verse. Guess what they put at the top of the list! You guessed it: Jeremiah 29:11. Really? I thought. I'm searching for

God's specific will for my life, and you're going to offer me a general promise that says God has a plan? I've heard that my entire life! I have it tattooed on my . . . just kidding. My church created an entire class around the topic that God has a specific plan for me—one that will lead to hope and a future. But what good is a hope and a future if I can't figure out how to get there? Or was that verse just for the nation of Israel? But I digress.

My skepticism at the Bible's ability to solve my dilemma grew, as did my skepticism of the website. I decided to give the list one more chance. After all, what other options did I have? It was well after midnight, and I was quickly approaching the point when I would once again give up on God's will to try again another day.

I read the second verse in the list: " . . . for this is *the will of God* in Christ Jesus for you." Wait a second! That's almost the exact phrase I've been waiting to find. I've been waiting for God to tell me, "Daniel, this is My will for you." I had been searching for God's will for as long as I could remember, and here, on the computer screen in front of me, was a verse offering God's will for *my* life. I kept reading. Actually, I decided to go to my Bible and read the entire New Testament letter of 1 Thessalonians.

> " . . . FOR THIS IS *THE WILL OF GOD* IN CHRIST JESUS FOR YOU."
> —1 THESSALONIANS 5:18

The first three chapters didn't mention anything about God's specific will for me, and I nearly gave up again. The excitement of thinking I had discovered God's will had faded, and I started to think it was just a random verse taken out of context. Then I read 1 Thessalonians 4, beginning in verse 3:

> For this is the will of God, your sanctification: that you abstain from sexual immorality; that each one of you know how to control his own body in holiness and honor, not in the passion of lust like the Gentiles who do not know God; that no one transgress and wrong his brother in this matter, because the Lord is an avenger in all these things, as we told you beforehand and solemnly warned you. For God has not called us for impurity, but in holiness. Therefore whoever disregards this, disregards not man but God, who gives his Holy Spirit to you. (1 Thessalonians 4:3–8 ESV)

Not only did 1 Thessalonians 4:3 mention the will of God, but the passage also included the very specific phrase "For God has not *called us*." In the same set of verses were both key phrases I was searching for—a description of *God's will* and *His calling*.

AHA!

On that night when I discovered these verses about God's will, my perspective on the call of God began to shift. In the unique and slightly Russian accent of Gru from *Despicable Me*: "Light bulb." It was a light-bulb moment.

Does that ever happen when you read Scripture? Have you ever been surprised to find something you had never noticed before in a passage you had read many times?

The longer I thought about this light-bulb moment and the

more I read and reread 1 Thessalonians 4, a hypothesis began to form in my brain: What if God's will is not about a career but about the way we live our lives? That deserves some more thought.

Now before we move on to the next chapter, I need to encourage you to be skeptical of my experience. Here's why. I just described an "aha" moment that I had when reading in 1 Thessalonians. The problem with "aha" moments is that we can sometimes jump to immediate conclusions about God based on one set of verses from one book in the much larger narrative of the Bible. That's never a good idea. Taking one verse out of context—like I did when I read Matthew 19 and concluded all the children should come to me—can be dangerous.

So now it's time for us to do some research, to actually test this new hypothesis that I'm going to call "common callings"— that God's will and calling are not about a specific career but are about the way we live our lives.

WHAT'S NEXT

1. What was your most recent "aha" moment with Scripture? What did you do to make sure that you were understanding it correctly and not just pulling it out of context for your moment of need?

2. As you continue to ask God, *What's next?*, consider starting a journal for Scripture and prayer. You can start with 1 Thessalonians 4:3–8. Write down truths that you see in the passage. Think about how they apply to your life and work. Pray for God to use His words in the Bible to help you figure out what's next.

8

COMMON CALLINGS

When you hear the word *calling*, what do you think of? I immediately think of a phone call. I dial some numbers into a magic black box that fits in my pocket, and somehow a phone in my friend's pocket on the other side of the room, city, or world rings. I know there's science behind it, but it sure sounds magical when you type it out.

People make phone calls for all sorts of reasons: to call in sick, to make an appointment, or to follow up after an interview. Sometimes a phone call is annoying because it's from someone we don't know, who bought our number off of a list we didn't sign up for and is using our number to try to sell us something (or worse, to endorse a political candidate). So not cool! Other times, we receive a phone call from a family member or friend, and we get excited to hear their voice and engage with them in conversation. As you read through this chapter, think of the word "call" in terms of a close friend calling to invite you to something.

Before the Bible as we know it existed, Paul wrote a lot of what is now the New Testament in the form of letters to various churches. Romans was written to the church in Rome. Galatians was written to the church in Galatia. First Thessalonians, which I was reading when I had my "aha" moment in the previous chapter, was the first of two letters written to the church in Thessalonica.

This would have been an "aha" moment for the Thessalonians too. At that time in history, Christianity was still relatively new and there were not many churches in the world. (I use the word *relatively* because the history of Christianity really begins in the ancient roots of Judaism.) There were copies of the Old Testament around, which could mostly be found in Jewish synagogues, but the books that would become the New Testament were just starting to be written. Everything people knew about Jesus they had learned firsthand from Jesus himself or secondhand from the apostles who had learned from Jesus. As a result, the teachings of Jesus were put into handwritten letters and then passed from church to church so everyone could learn from them. Paul not only met Jesus in a really fascinating encounter that you have to read to believe (Acts 9), but Paul also spent a lot of time with Jesus's disciples.

The Thessalonians already knew the basics of the Jesus story, because Paul told them in person at some point in the past (1 Thessalonians 2:2). Paul—as a friend, mentor, and leader of the church—is following up his in-person teachings with a written letter to expound on how the Jesus story impacts the way they should live.

CHARACTER, NOT CAREER

In the previous chapter, we looked at a section of Paul's letter to the Thessalonians where God's will and His calling are not described in terms of career—as we've so often been taught—but in terms of character. Let's look at that section again:

> For this is the *will of God, your* sanctification. . . . For God has not *called us* for impurity, but in holiness. Therefore whoever disregards this, disregards not man but God, who gives his Holy Spirit to you. (1 Thessalonians 4:3–8 ESV)

The word "called" here means something similar to when someone dials your phone number. The Greek root word is *kaléō*, but you don't even need to know that to understand what Paul is saying in his letter. In the same way that someone calls you on the phone to invite you to do something, the word *called* in the Bible simply means to invite or summon.

So here's the question: What was Paul telling the Thessalonians—and now everyone who reads the Bible—that God has invited us to do? He's invited believers to a new identity in Him—to holiness. The apostle Peter also wrote about this in a letter to believers: As God "who *called* you is holy, be holy yourselves in all your conduct; for it is written, 'You shall be holy, for I am holy'" (1 Peter 1:15–16). What does the word *holy* mean? To be set apart. What does it mean to be set apart? The rest of 1 Thessalonians offers some answers to that question. In 1 Thessalonians 5, for example, we are told

- to show respect to pastors and our spiritual fathers and esteem them highly (vv. 12–13);

- to be at peace with everyone (v. 13);

- to encourage the fainthearted, help the weak, and be patient with all (v. 14); and

- to do good to everyone, even those who do evil (v. 15).

Again, as far as I can tell, Paul is not saying God has called or invited the Thessalonians to a certain job but has instead invited them into a certain way of living.

Before we move on to some other examples of "calling" in the Bible, I want to make sure we don't lose sight of a connection that Paul makes in the verses we looked at above. Paul connects God's calling—His invitation—to God's will for our lives. I think most of us would agree that when we are searching for God's calling, we are also searching for God's will. This is important because as we look through the rest of 1 Thessalonians, and then on to other sections of Scripture, I want us to be looking not only for the use of the words *call* or *calling* but also for passages that specifically describe God's *will* for our lives.

Here's a great example that we will dive into in the next chapter: "Rejoice always, pray without ceasing, give thanks in all circumstances; for this is the *will of God* in Christ Jesus for you" (1 Thessalonians 5:16–18). Instead of a specific call to a specific job, Paul wrote that God's will for the Thessalonians includes rejoicing, praying, and giving thanks regardless of the circumstances. Evidently, God has called them to a life characterized by joy, prayer, and thankfulness. So far the hypothesis—that God's calling and will are not to a certain job but to a certain way of living—is holding up.

DEDICATION, NOT DREAM JOB

The word *kaléō* shows up in various forms 148 times in the New Testament, which means we have a whole bunch of examples we can look at to see how the word is used. Because of that, we can discover what my seminary professors described as "the breadth of meaning." In other words, we get to see the word used in so many different ways that we get a picture of all the different ways it *can* be used. Let's take our hypothesis and look at some more uses of the word *called*.

"See what love the Father has given to us, that we should be *called* children of God; and that is what we are" (1 John 3:1). Here's another letter in which calling is described in terms unrelated to what we do for a job. It's important to note that Paul didn't write this letter, which means another apostle seemed to use the word *kaléō* in a way that described something other than a job.

"We know that all things work together for good for those who love God, who are called according to his purpose" (Romans 8:28). Skip the first half of the verse for now—here Paul suggests God has "called" us according to His purpose. I think the word "summoned" might be better here, but it fits with Paul's use of the word in 1 Thessalonians and doesn't have anything to do with a job (that we can tell).

In other parts of Romans, Paul uses the word *called* several times, and some of these uses can be both confusing and controversial. For example: "And those whom he predestined he also called, and those whom he called he also justified, and those whom he justified he also glorified" (Romans 8:30). This is what I call a "landmine" verse because different denominations interpret it *very* differently. I'm not going to get into the controversial aspects of the verse, but I do want to point out the use of the word *called*. Both sides of interpretation of this verse seem to agree that Paul is using the word to suggest God invites people into relationship with Him. God loves us so much that He's inviting us to be adopted into His family. Again, the use of calling has nothing to do with a job.

Here are a few other ways the word is used. We are called

- into the fellowship of God's Son (1 Corinthians 1:9);
- to peace (1 Corinthians 7:15; Colossians 3:15);
- to freedom (Galatians 5:13); and
- out of darkness and into God's light (1 Peter 2:9).

Are you starting to get a feel for how the word *called* is used in the Bible? I think it's fascinating that so far none of the references mention anything about a career or a job or even mission or ministry. The title of this chapter is "Common Callings."

For a long time now, Christian leaders have emphasized the specific call of God on a person's life. When I began to research this in the Bible, I discovered a stack of passages and verses that described general callings for all Christians. Look at the short list we just made. There are not specific individuals called to peace—God has invited all Christians to experience peace and be peacemakers. There are not specific individuals called to freedom—God has invited all of us to a life of freedom. These are *common* callings—invitations for all people who hear God's voice and respond.

WHAT'S NEXT

1. The word *call* means to invite or summon. Read 1 Corinthians 1:26–31. "Consider your own call," it says. How do these verses relate to your own call to salvation through faith in Jesus Christ?

2. Go back through the examples in this chapter and think about what it means to be invited by God into these things. How should that impact the way we live?

9

DIGGING DEEPER

I want to encourage you to be skeptical. (It's a surprisingly useful life skill!)

Of the 148 uses of the word *kaléō* in the New Testament, so far we've only looked at 10. This is like a long major league baseball season (which is currently 162 games long), and the "called-to-a-career team" has started 0–10 (no wins, 10 losses). It doesn't mean they can't rally and still make the playoffs. So let's dig a little deeper.

RESEARCHING THE WORD *CALLED*

In Hebrews (which may or may not have been written by Paul—no one knows for sure), there's an interesting passage about being a priest in ancient Judaism. The priest is in charge of things pertaining to people's relationship with God—no pressure! Specifically, a priest was responsible for the gifts and sacrifices the people brought. The guidelines for offering sacrifices were detailed and complicated, and the priest had to offer sacrifices to cover sins for the people as well as for himself. The passage implies that the position should make him humble rather than prideful. So how does this relate to the topic of "calling"? Hebrews 5:4 indicates that someone should not become a priest unless they are *called* by God: "And one does not presume to take this honor, but takes it only when called by God, just as Aaron was." (Moses's brother Aaron was the first official priest of Israel.) The invitation described in this example is a specific calling of God to a specific job. The called-to-a-career team has just won their first game, and their record is now 1–10.

Here's another example that can probably be stretched to help out the called-to-a-career team, but it's a little fishy (yes, this is a pun). According to Mark, Jesus "called" the disciples to follow Him and become fishers of people (1:16–20). I think the argument could be made that Jesus called them to a new job as disciples, though they wouldn't be paid for this promotion. (And it eventually became a common calling as all of us are called to be fishers of people—to tell them the good news about how much God loves them.) We'll give this one to the called-to-a-career team as well, and now the record is 2–10.

There's another example in Mark 3:13. Jesus looked out over all the people who were following Him—which was a lot—and "called" the twelve disciples to himself. Then He "appointed" them as apostles (3:13, 16). You could argue that this is a "call" to a new career as a professional Jesus-follower. The record is now 3–10.

The final note I want to make about the called-to-a-career team is in mentioning a section of verses that describes how God gives people certain gifts to be used to encourage the church. But remember, we have to read this section knowing Moses was called by God to do something that fell outside of his giftedness. One of the most common references used to prove that God calls people to ministry is Ephesians 4:11–12: "The gifts he gave were that some would be apostles, some prophets, some evangelists, some pastors and teachers, to equip the saints for the work of ministry, for building up the body of Christ." Notice that neither the word *called* nor the idea of *God's will* are mentioned in this passage, but let's be generous and grant this to the called-to-a-career team and update their record to 4–10.

In this same letter to the church at Corinth, however, Paul has a lot more to say about *calling*, and those references are all wins for the called-to-a-way-of-living team. (I'll update the win–loss record as we go):

> I therefore, the prisoner in the Lord, beg you to lead a life worthy of the *calling* [4–11] to which you have been *called* [4–12], with all humility and gentleness, with patience, bearing with one another in love, making every effort to maintain the unity of the Spirit in the bond of peace. There is one body and one Spirit, just as you were *called* [4–13] to the one hope of your *calling* [4–14], one Lord, one faith, one baptism, one God and Father of all, who is above all and through all and in all. (Ephesians 4:1–6)

In these six verses, we have *calling* or *called* used four times, and it doesn't once mention a job or a career. What is God inviting us to in this passage? We are called, through the power and influence of the Holy Spirit, to be humble, gentle, patient, and loving, with the goal of promoting unity among brothers and sisters in Christ.

What if we took this calling as seriously as we take the desire to discover a dream job? What if we woke up every day and asked God to help us live up to His invitation to be humble in our interactions with others—lifting up their interests above our own? What if we set out each day to be gentle toward people who are rude or impatient with us? What does it look like to "bear with one another in love," and what if we tried our best to do it? Can you or I say that we are "making every effort" to pursue unity and hold out a handshake of peace even to our enemies? I don't know about you, but this passage alone is challenging enough. If I were to take it seriously, I'd spend all my energy focusing on the call of God to be a peacemaker and wouldn't have time to worry about what I did for a living.

If you look up the rest of the New Testament passages in which a form of *kaléō* is used, the final record between the called-by-God-to-a-career team and the called-by-God-to-a-way-of-living team is 4–145 (remember, we gave the career team a win for a passage that doesn't mention the word *calling*, which is why we have 149 total games even though *kaléō* is only used 148 times). I'm going to go out on a limb and suggest that the called-by-God-to-a-career team didn't make the playoffs. In fact, they may want to go ahead and begin restructuring the team, starting with the manager. Maybe calling is not all they've made it out to be.

I'm not saying that God doesn't invite people to do specific things. The stories of Moses and Jonah prove otherwise. The Hebrews passage suggests that God once called certain people to be priests. Jesus called the disciples to follow Him, and they ultimately became the apostles who dedicated themselves to teaching the good news of Jesus to the world as missionaries. Yet even this deserves one qualifier—Paul, one of the apostles, was a tent-maker by trade and a missionary by lifestyle (Acts 18).

What I *am* suggesting, however, is that the weight of the Scriptures points us toward something much more important than what we do for a living. Remember when I shared with you the story about my calling class? I described the A-team and the B-team, those called by God to a career in ministry and those who weren't called by God to a career in ministry. Ephesians shows us that there's only one team—those called by God to live a life worthy of the calling to which we have been called. All of us—stockers, teachers, baristas, and pastors, employed, underemployed, or unemployed—are all called to lives of humility, gentleness, patience, unity, peace, and love. And that's where the will of God comes in.

> THE WEIGHT OF THE SCRIPTURES POINTS US TOWARD SOMETHING MUCH MORE IMPORTANT THAN WHAT WE DO FOR A LIVING.

RESEARCHING THE PHRASE *WILL OF GOD*

My serendipitous discovery from 1 Thessalonians inspired me to search the Bible for not only verses about God's calling but also other verses about God's will. The two go hand-in-hand: many of us are searching for God's calling on our lives because we want to know what His will is. And so I found some verses that specifically describe God's will:

1 Thessalonians 5:16–18: "Rejoice always, pray without ceasing, give thanks in all circumstances; *for this is the will of God in Christ Jesus for you.*" Although these verses do not tell us what career to pursue, all of these verses describe how we should act in whatever job we have today. Even if you are in a job you don't like, God has called you to rejoice always and give thanks in all circumstances. I don't know about you, but that's quite a challenge for me. It's a challenge for all of us who are asking "What's next?" Even in our seasons of uncertainty, we are called to rejoice and give thanks. To trust that God has us exactly where we are supposed to be. To look for things, even now, to be thankful for.

Gratitude is a powerful antidote for discontentment. If you are frustrated because things aren't working out the way you desire, try thanking God and rejoicing in every little thing. Maybe start a gratitude journal. I know it's frustrating not to know what you want to do with your life, or to know what you want to do but find it unattainable. But even now, try thanking God for where you are, for whatever paycheck you get, for the friends with whom He's surrounded you. Thank God for positive interactions with customers or coworkers. Consider each day a practice session for the future, and thank God for the opportunity to practice His will even outside of the perfect job. I think you'll find gratitude to be life-changing.

1 Peter 2:15: "For it is *God's will* that by doing right you should silence the ignorance of the foolish." If you read the context for this verse you discover God's calling to "do right" is an invitation to be honorable (v. 12); to respect and submit to authority (vv. 13–14); to live as people who are free to serve God (v. 16); to honor everyone, love fellow believers, and fear God

(v. 17). Again, nothing about a specific job, but a whole bunch of things that build character.

Doing right is also a powerful antidote for discontentment. Even if you are in a seemingly dead-end job or in a job you don't consider a dream job, you have opportunities to do right—to respect authority, honor others, and love people. Even if you are sitting in a class that seems like a waste of time, you have a chance to submit to the authority who is making you take the class and to help those around you. I won't say it will be easy, but if you practice doing the right things even in tough situations, you will find that discontentment dissipates as you feel the joy of doing what God would want for you to do.

Not only does doing right make you feel better, but if you do what's right—even in tough situations—you will also be the first person in line for promotions and raises. And here's a thought: you never know whom you are serving. You could end up handing a burger to your next boss—a guy or gal who runs a company in which there is a job that is a perfect fit for you. When you hand them a burger in the right way—with a good attitude, respectful tone, and caring smile—you will stand out among your peers. So not only is doing right a powerful antidote to discontentment, but it also sets you up for future success.

Ephesians 5:15–20:

> Be careful then how you live, not as unwise people but as wise, making the most of the time, because the days are evil. So do not be foolish, *but understand what the will of the Lord is.* Do not get drunk with wine, for that is debauchery; but be filled with

the Spirit, as you sing psalms and hymns and spiritual songs among yourselves, singing and making melody to the Lord in your hearts, giving thanks to God the Father at all times and for everything in the name of our Lord Jesus Christ.

Ephesians 5 talks about how God's followers should act. We should be loving (v. 2), thankful (vv. 4), and Spirit-filled (v. 18) instead of impure (v. 3), vulgar (v. 4), greedy (v. 5), or drunk (v. 18). People who understand the Lord's will (v. 17) will be wise (v. 15) instead of foolish (v. 17).

Wisdom is yet another powerful antidote to discontentment. When we go through life disgruntled, irritable, impatient, frustrated, bored, or unmotivated, oftentimes we make ourselves suffer just as much as we make those around us suffer. More than that, we also make stupid decisions—like responding in anger to a coworker, doing sloppy work, or walking out of a job without giving notice. Those decisions can follow us for a long time. When a potential new employer calls the old job for a reference, how do you think that conversation will go? Not so well. Wisdom keeps us from letting our discontentment ruin our lives.

None of these passages that detail God's will for us has anything to do with a specific job or occupation. Do you realize what this means? For me it means God's will for my life was not for me to become an Air Force pilot or an FBI agent. For you it means that God's will is not about becoming a [*fill in the blank*]. God's will is for you and me to be wise. God's will for us is to encourage others with songs about who God is and what He has done for us. (How cool is that? God's will is for us to sing and make music!) God's explicit and detailed calling on your life and my life is for us to be full of gratitude for everything He has done for us and to honor and respect others in the name of Jesus. Wow! God has a very specific will for our lives, but it doesn't look much like what we expected.

> GOD HAS A VERY SPECIFIC WILL
> FOR OUR LIVES, BUT IT DOESN'T LOOK
> MUCH LIKE WHAT WE EXPECTED.

When I first collected these examples and explored the use of the word "calling" and the phrase "God's will" in Scripture, a question popped up: How had I missed all these truths before? I had searched for God's will and calling for so long, and it was right in front of me the entire time. How did I not see it? I think our Western culture has so overemphasized the pursuit of a career, that we—as individuals and church leaders—have been focused on the wrong things. We've been so focused on discovering God's *specific* call to a particular job that we have missed God's will for our lives—or at best, we've neglected it. In a culture that promotes significance through what you do for a living, we've sacrificed the call of God for our own call.

Instead of rejoicing always and giving thanks in every circumstance, we complain on social media about our bosses and coworkers.

Instead of accepting God's invitation to patience, we try to make things happen and end up stressed over things we can't control.

Instead of humbly accepting our roles in an organization with the knowledge that we matter because we're a child of

God, we pursue more and more, hoping that we can find significance in a career.

Over the next few chapters we will further explore God's will through examining some of these common callings, and I think you will agree with me that God's calling is to something so much better than a job. Remember how we defined the dream job as a job that offers fulfillment and purpose? We are getting ready to discover some really good news—that fulfillment and purpose don't depend on what we do for a living and they are available to us today.

WHAT'S NEXT

1. Do you find freedom in the fact that God's call on and will for your life is not connected to a job? Are there any particular verses in this chapter that stand out to you?

2. Which of the passages about God's will was most challenging to you—1 Thessalonians 5:16–18; 1 Peter 2:15; or Ephesians 5:15–20? Journal and pray over the passage, and ask God to help you accomplish His will.

10

A LIFE THAT MATTERS

Two groups of men, who would normally be in conflict with one another, were more focused on a verbal assault against someone they both viewed as a threat. These were men of influence and prestige—the leading religious scholars of the day. They were brilliant thinkers, and they spent much of their time debating answers to questions regular people didn't even know to ask.

Normally, the air would be full of loud arguing as the two groups met in public to disagree on deep, philosophically based religious issues. They liked to have the crowds watch them argue, because it was another opportunity to further distinguish themselves as men of brilliance. They enjoyed bringing up impossible situations and unanswerable questions so they could watch the opposing scholars squirm to provide an intelligible answer. It was like a game to them—to see if they could create a question for which *any* answer would be wrong.

Over the previous few years, the two groups had watched as a small-town teacher rose in popularity and influence. At first, the scholars listened in jealous appreciation of the wisdom of the no-name rabbi. In fact, some of the scholars had been around twenty or so years earlier, when this man—then a young boy—sat in the synagogue and reasoned with them at a level well beyond His years. At that time, they were so impressed with Him that they thought for sure He would grow up to become one of them—to one day share a seat of influence. The young man never had a chance to pursue scholarship, however. Instead, His father apprenticed Him to be a stonemason and woodworker.

Years later, the religious scholars were amazed to see this young carpenter and stonemason—now an adult—travel the countryside with an entourage of disciples and fans. They appreciated a lot of what He taught, and they enjoyed a few sermons He preached.

Unfortunately for them, however, the man slowly became too influential, and soon He threatened the influence and power of the two groups of religious scholars. There were a few instances in which this guy had presented His audience with statements that flirted with flat-out blasphemy. It soon became clear that the scholars needed to discredit Him and remind the crowd that He was still a small-town simpleton who really didn't know what He was talking about.

They thought it would be easy. After a quick meeting, one of the groups came up with a question they knew would trip Him up, and they picked the best person to deliver the question. He was a lawyer who made his living by trapping people in webs of questioning. He was a master at asking impossible questions and watching the accused—whether guilty or innocent—fade under the weight of accusation and guilt.

"Teacher," the lawyer started in a respectful and flattering tone, "what is the greatest commandment in all of the law? If one of the simpler minds listening to us today was only able to keep one commandment, which commandment should he focus on?" (See Matthew 22:36.)

The lawyer nearly walked away, confident he had won. Israel's law—in its entirety—was the most sacred part of Jewish history and culture. Everyone was dedicated to following the law. The law of Moses was the supreme code of the land, and no parts of it could be separated from the rest. No commandment could be greater than any other commandment. Finally, the crowd would see Jesus for the false teacher He was and would desert Him. The lawyer looked at Jesus and smirked— the same smirk he showed defendants in the courtroom.

Jesus looked back at the lawyer, but without so much as a hint of condemnation or anger. In fact, the lawyer was surprised to see compassion and kindness in Jesus's eyes. But he also noticed something else: Jesus's eyes were filled with a fiery confidence—as if He had known the question ahead of time and was prepared with a passionate response. Clearly, Jesus knew what the lawyer was up to, and He knew He could answer the question. Yet He still somehow cared about the lawyer who tried to trap Him. How Jesus communicated all of this through one look, the lawyer didn't know. The closest he had come to a similar experience was the way his mom looked at him when he was in trouble—a unique combination of love and stern discipline. He began to feel uncomfortable as Jesus responded:

> "You shall love the Lord your God with all your heart, and with all your soul, and with all your mind." This is the greatest and first commandment. And a second is like it: "You shall love your neighbor

as yourself." On these two commandments hang all
the law and the prophets. (Matthew 22:37–40)

Jesus, in a moment of being questioned about the Law, sum-
marized all of God's expectations in just a few short sentences.
Like a thesis-driven paper for school, the Greatest Commandment and the One Like It are the summary statements of God's
expectations for our lives. They give purpose to life, and they
lead to true fulfillment. I figure that's probably a good place
for us to start as we attempt to discover God's will and calling
for our lives.

THE GREATEST COMMANDMENTS

Jesus's response to the Pharisees on that day was not something
He made up on the spot. It wasn't an off-the-cuff response.
Jesus didn't create a new commandment to answer the lawyer's
question. He was quoting from two different places within the
law of Moses.

The first part of Jesus's response came from something called
the *Sh'ma*.[1] Like the preambles to the constitutions of countries
like the United States and the Republic of Rwanda or to the
Declaration of the Rights of Man and of the Citizen in French law,
or the many other foundational statements that summarize the
purpose and mission of various sovereign nations, the *Sh'ma* is
the defining statement of the law of Moses. For the nation of
Israel and the Jews, the *Sh'ma* is a big deal; it unifies them as
one people under one God.

The passage Jesus quoted—Deuteronomy 6:4–5—is
called the *Sh'ma* because that's the first word of the passage,
and it means "hear." This call to *hear* is used several times in

Deuteronomy. It's like a parent calling their child to pay attention to what they're about to say, like "Listen up!" In a similar way to teaching my son to wash his hands and not to lick a restaurant window (don't ask), God teaches His kids principles designed for their good. In the *Sh'ma*, God asks the children of Israel—His children—to listen to His teaching. Also like a parent, God asks His children to do something—they were not only to hear the truth but also to respond to it.

And what were they to respond to? A call to love God with all that they are: heart, soul, and might. It is the foundation for Moses's law—the preamble—the cornerstone on which all of Israel's covenant history with God is founded.

The second part of Jesus's response came from Leviticus 19. Leviticus is a very long list of things the Israelites were taught to do and not do. The list is so long, it would be hard to memorize them all and even harder to obey. Yet within this long list of things to do and not do, we find the phrase, "love you neighbor as yourself" (19:18).

Jesus is teaching that this is the key phrase of all the laws that surround it, and if you look at the rules that surround the phrase it becomes clear why this is such a compelling summary. Look at Leviticus 19:9–10, for example. God tells the Israelites not to harvest to the edges of their lands or to strip the vineyard clean of grapes. Instead, God wants them to leave the edges of the field and the leftover grapes for the poor and immigrants. In other words, God wants the Israelites to "love their neighbors" by providing food for them.

It's no wonder the Pharisees marveled at Jesus's response and no longer wanted to ask Him questions. Like a pastor who takes two passages of Scripture and draws between them a valid and powerful connection you and I hadn't noticed before, Jesus brought the audience back to the two foundational principles of their purpose and mission as a nation and a "people." Love God and love others.

SIMPLE FREEDOM

Jesus takes what was a burden—the weight of a complicated law code—and makes it simple. As an American, I think about the Constitution and how complicated it is, especially now. There are people who spend their lives studying the intricacies of what has become an extremely complex system of laws and amendments. Wouldn't it be great if Jesus would come to simplify our laws (or at least our tax system!) down to two simple principles?

More than just simplifying the law for the Jews and answering the unanswerable question of the prestigious lawyer, I think Jesus was also saying something to the rest of the audience—to the people standing around that day, and to us today. I think it's reasonable to assume that God's expectations for everyone, even those of us who are not Israelites, are so much simpler than we make them out to be. (Notice I didn't use the word *easier*.) Everything you and I read in the Bible—every story, passage, and verse—is summed up in two simple commands, the greatest commands, to love God and to love others.

> EVERYTHING YOU AND I READ IN THE BIBLE—EVERY STORY, PASSAGE, AND VERSE—IS SUMMED UP IN TWO SIMPLE COMMANDS, THE GREATEST COMMANDS, TO LOVE GOD AND TO LOVE OTHERS.

It's really important for us to consider this story at this point in our journey of discovering what God's calling and will are for our lives. We've already covered quite a bit of ground and we've mentioned several common callings. Be humble, patient, gentle, and holy. Pursue peace and unity. Lead a life worthy of the life to which you have been called. And there are so many more that we haven't discussed yet. Imagine if each of these callings represented a book from the library, and you were filling a backpack with books that described the ways to discover and live a successful life. The bag is getting full already, isn't it?

A relationship with God can seem like a heavy burden because it's full of so many expectations of how God wants us to live. If we take the message of this book seriously—that God's calling is not about a specific job but about a specific way of living—we could easily get overwhelmed by the number of things God wants us to do for Him. If we are feeling overwhelmed by the pressure to perform in order to make God happy, we are missing the point.

Jesus's response to the lawyer brings freedom and hope to us, too. Walking with God and stepping into your calling is not about doing anything for God but is about being loved by God and loving Him in return. It's about being in a relationship with Him. Period.

Remember one of the first "callings" we discussed from 1 John 3:1? God loves us so much that He's calling us to become His kids. It's like we've been orphaned our whole lives, until we suddenly realize God has invited us to be a part of His family. He's at the courthouse with an offer of adoption, and all we have to say is "Yes!" This is so much better than just an invitation to a dream job.

We thought that God's will for and calling on our lives

would be to a career, but in reality God's invitation is to a long-lasting and dependable relationship with Him. Instead of a just a dream job, God's will is for us to experience a dream life—to be loved and cared for by the greatest Father who always gets it right.

The greatest commandment or the greatest common calling is the same invitation expressed in 1 John. God loves us and invites us to love Him back. Take all the books out of your backpack. Take away all of the expectations about what you think it looks like to please God; and for now, simply rest in God's love for you. In a world full of religions that tell us to do stuff, how freeing is it to hear God say, "I already love you"? In a world full of pressure to pursue a dream job so our lives might matter, feel the freedom of hearing God say, "You already matter to me."

WHAT'S NEXT

1. Do you believe that God loves you? Why or why not?

2. What does it look like to love God in return?

11

DISCOVERING PURPOSE AND FULFILLMENT

Hank didn't have a choice. He had been out of work for several months, had already lost his house to foreclosure, and was struggling to provide food for his wife and kids. Every job Hank applied for had fallen through, except one. He had been offered an executive-level position with a small factory based in the middle of a violent neighborhood. If Hank took the job, he would be commuting through a bad area of town.

But it was worse. When Hank lost his previous job, he also lost both of his cars. His primary transportation was a company vehicle that had been taken away when he was laid off. His second car—a van he had purchased—was repossessed when Hank could no longer make payments. He was left with only his mountain bike—a very nice one—as a mode of transportation. Not only would Hank be commuting through the violent neighborhood but he would be riding a nice mountain bike while wearing an executive style suit and tie. Can you say "set-up for a mugging"?

Hank was afraid. But what other choice did he have? If he was going to take care of his family, he needed this job.

One early morning on the way to work in thick fog, Hank was attacked. He barely saw the guy coming. By the time he noticed the look of aggression in the man's face, it was too late. Hank was mugged, stripped, and left alongside the curb with a gaping knife wound in his left side. He tried to call out for help, but just taking a deep breath so he could talk proved too painful.

Hank drifted in and out of consciousness. After what seemed like forever, a figure emerged from the fog. The man got close enough for Hank to see a cross around his neck and Christian tracts in his hands. *It's going to be okay*, Hank thought, just as he blacked out.

What Hank didn't see because he went unconscious was that the man—a businessman and street evangelist—nearly stepped on him. When he finally saw Hank, he felt compassion for him, but noticing that Hank had been stabbed, he became more concerned about his own safety than Hank's rescue. He left, quickly.

After the evangelist disappeared, a woman wearing a priestly collar crossed the street. Watching for oncoming traffic in the fog, she tripped over Hank's unconscious body. Stunned and embarrassed, she stood up, dusted herself off, and quickly walked away.

Suddenly, the air was filled with the loud screeching of brakes and tires on asphalt. A yellow van stopped within inches of Hank's head.

The Middle-Eastern cabdriver got out of his vehicle and

rushed to Hank's side. He ripped off his shirt and did the best he could to stop the bleeding. He picked up Hank and placed him in one of the captain's chairs in the middle section of the taxi. Then he drove as fast as he could to the hospital a few blocks away.

The driver stopped at the emergency entrance and frantically called for help. He stood aside as medics responded, and soon Hank was being rushed to surgery.

The driver surveyed his van. Blood was soaked into the seat; there'd be no more fares until that was cleaned anyway, and he was concerned about the man in surgery. He parked his taxi, grabbed his jacket to cover his undershirt, and went inside to wait.

A few hours later, the doctor came out to let the cabdriver know that the man he rescued would be okay. The hospital had made some inquiries. "His name's Hank, and he works at the furniture factory up the street. Unfortunately, he's still in the probationary period and doesn't have insurance yet."

"If he doesn't have insurance, how is he going to pay?" the driver asked.

"We'll figure that out later. I'm sure his job is steady enough that he can make payments. But that's more information than I should have shared. I need to run."

The Middle-Eastern cabdriver had been working in the United States for years and, without a family to support, he had saved up quite a bit of money. He drove to the bank, withdrew $10,000 from his account, and drove back to the hospital.

He took the cash to the billing desk. "This should help pay for a lot of what you've done so far," he said. "I will be back in a few days to check on him. At that time, I can pay for what's left." As you can imagine, the man left the hospital with a deep sense of fulfillment—he had made a difference in someone's life.

Two thousand-ish years ago, Jesus told a story similar to that of the Middle-Eastern taxi driver. Here's a quick summary so you can see what I mean: One day, robbers attacked a man traveling between two cities and left him for dead at the side of the road. A priest and a Levite—two Jewish religious leaders—saw the bloodied man but refused to help him. Eventually, a Samaritan saw the man and saved his life. He generously covered all the man's expenses.

In order for us to understand this story and why Jesus told it, we need to consider its context.

One day, a lawyer stepped up to test Jesus, and asked: "Teacher, what must I do to inherit eternal life?" But instead of directly answering the question, Jesus asked him a question: "What does the law say?"

The lawyer responded, "You shall love the Lord your God with all your heart, and with all your soul, and with all your strength, and with all your mind; and your neighbor as yourself" (Luke 10:27). Sounds a lot like the last chapter, doesn't it?

"That's right," Jesus responded. "Do this and you will live."

"But who is my neighbor?" the lawyer asked.

Jesus, in the brilliant way only He could, answered the man by telling him the story we know as the parable of the good Samaritan. The story is more than that of one man helping another in desperate need. It is a story full of nuance, and the hero of the story ends up being a perceived enemy of Israel. You see, the Jews of Jesus's time did not like the Samaritans but considered them traitors and half-breeds. The Samaritans' racial lineage wasn't pure, and they tried to worship God outside of

Jerusalem. Yet a Samaritan, not a priest and not a Levite, was the hero of Jesus's story.

LOVE YOUR NEIGHBOR

Jesus is pushing the lawyer—and us—into uncomfortable territory as we consider what it looks like to love a neighbor. In this story, Jesus is suggesting that someone considered racially and religiously inferior may be more in tune with the heart and desires of God than accepted religious leaders. That's the reason I picked a Middle-Eastern man as the hero in Hank's story. Many Americans will look on Middle Easterners with suspicion. Who are the people you look down on simply because of their appearance or religious beliefs? Are there any groups you feel uncomfortable around?

I don't want us to get lost in a discussion about race or religion, however, because the story is not just about prejudice. Jesus's primary point is to answer the lawyer's question—Who is my neighbor?—and its implied follow-up question—And what does it look like to love my neighbor?

Biblical scholar Darrell Bock puts Jesus's answer in these terms:

> Jesus' point is, simply be a neighbor. Do not rule out certain people as neighbors. And his parable makes the point emphatically by providing a model from a group the lawyer has probably excluded as possible neighbors.
>
> To love God means to show mercy to those in need. An authentic life is found in serving God and caring for others. . . . Neighbors are not determined

by race, creed or gender; neighbors consist of anyone
in need made in the image of God.[1]

You and I—regardless of what job we have or what school we attend—are surrounded by people in need who are made in the image of God, and every person who's made in the image of God is a neighbor.

It's easy for us to see friends and family as made in the image of God. It's easy for us to see some of our coworkers as made in the image of God. But in the story of the Good Samaritan, Jesus is not only pressing the audience to examine their prejudices, but He's addressing something else that He teaches in several places throughout the Gospels. It's an invitation that examines what it looks like to love our neighbor, and—just a heads-up—we're not going to like this very much.

LOVE YOUR ENEMY

Here's what Jesus says in a story that is found just a few short chapters before the parable of the Good Samaritan:

> But to you who are listening I say: Love your enemies, do good to those who hate you, bless those who curse you, pray for those who mistreat you. If someone slaps you on one cheek, turn to them the other also. If someone takes your coat, do not withhold your shirt from them. Give to everyone who asks you, and if anyone takes what belongs to you, do not demand it back. Do to others as you would have them do to you.
>
> If you love those who love you, what credit is that to you? Even sinners love those who love them.

And if you do good to those who are good to you, what credit is that to you? Even sinners do that. And if you lend to those from whom you expect repayment, what credit is that to you? Even sinners lend to sinners, expecting to be repaid in full. But love your enemies, do good to them, and lend to them without expecting to get anything back. Then your reward will be great, and you will be children of the Most High, because he is kind to the ungrateful and wicked. Be merciful, just as your Father is merciful. (Luke 6:27–36 NIV)

Who comes to mind when you read the command "Love your enemies"? Maybe several names leap to mind, along with memories you wish you could forget. Or no names at all, because you haven't been in a fight since second grade and you can't even remember that kid's name. Either way, the concept of loving enemies seems difficult. No one should have to put up with being mistreated, should they?

A few months ago, a woman came into our family-owned entertainment center and asked to speak with a manager. As I approached her, I could tell she was angry. I took a deep breath and walked up to her with a smile.

The woman started berating me because, at one point, a Bible verse had been painted on a wall and she wanted to know why the owners had abandoned their faith and given in to the culture war (quite a few assumptions here, huh?). I tried to explain to her that the wall was one of several that had been removed. The remodel had nothing to do with what was painted on the wall. She wouldn't have it. She verbally attacked me, my family, my faith—all of it.

All of us run into people who mistreat us. For some of us, it happens just about every day at work, whether it's by a coworker, a boss, or—as in the case of the unreasonable Bible lady—a customer. Sometimes we are mistreated physically; other times, emotionally. Yet Jesus is inviting us to love those who mistreat us—to be a neighbor, even to those who are unreasonable. And in a work setting, this can happen a lot!

To be honest, I don't like this common calling. My human nature yells out in opposition to God on this one. I don't want the people I don't like to be in heaven. Like Jonah, I don't want those who do bad stuff to find forgiveness. If they've caused others to suffer, I want them to suffer. I want to call out to God and tell Him, "Lord, you obviously don't understand." Yet Jesus calls us to love our enemies, and if we fast-forward to the end of Jesus's life on earth we see that He didn't ask us to do something He wasn't willing to do himself. On the cross, Jesus forgave those who brutally beat Him with rods and whips and those who pounded nails into His hands and feet. Jesus loved His enemies. And if Jesus can love His enemies—who did way worse things to Him than I've ever experienced—I think He can challenge the lawyer to celebrate the heroism of the Good Samaritan and can call us to love all of our neighbors—even those we don't like.

This might mean forgiving someone who has literally slapped me or stolen my stuff. It meant looking at the angry Bible lady and trying to imagine what had happened to her earlier in the day to cause her to act this way. I encourage my staff to do the same thing—to assume that the person must have already had a terrible day and is taking it out on the wrong person (ahem, me). Maybe this customer had been attacked on social media for posting a verse of encouragement. Maybe she had just watched the news and heard someone talk about how a group was suing a Christian business owner for having the Ten Commandments posted on the wall. Maybe she had a car accident on the way to our business or found out her daughter was diagnosed with cancer. None of this justifies the lady's mistreatment of me or my staff, but discovering someone's story can often help us look on others, even someone who mistreats us, with compassion. I wish I could say I always respond this way. (Just an FYI: A few hours after the incident, someone radioed for me to come upstairs; Bible-lady wanted to talk to me again. I braced myself for what I was sure would be another confrontation. Do you know what happened? She apologized and gave me a hug! I wish confrontation always ended that way!)

Now, I know some who read this chapter might be thinking, "Great stories, Daniel. But what does this have to do with discovering what's next? How does this relate to what I do for a living? What does this have to do with discovering God's calling on my life, when, after all the word *calling* doesn't even show up in the second greatest commandment?" Great questions.

WHAT'S LOVE GOT TO DO WITH IT?

Paul, in a letter to the churches in Galatia, writes:

> You, my brothers and sisters, were *called* to be free. But do not use your freedom to indulge the flesh; rather, serve one another humbly in love. For the entire law is fulfilled in keeping this one command: "Love your neighbor as yourself." (Galatians 5:13–14 NIV)

Although Jesus didn't use the word *called*, Paul did. He suggests that the second greatest commandment is one of our invitations into God's will. Earlier in the book, we discussed our desire to discover a career that is both purposeful and fulfilling. Our purpose and fulfillment isn't going to be found in "indulging the flesh" as this passage says; it's going to be found in this calling—the invitation to love others.

Consider this: What if your purpose and my purpose is not in what we do for a career, but in "serving one another"—seen in the way we treat coworkers, customers, or bosses? What if true fulfillment doesn't come from finding the perfect job, but from using *any* job as a platform for humbly serving those around us?

In Hank's story, the Middle-Eastern hero drove a taxicab. As the storyteller in that scenario, I can assure you that driving a cab wasn't his dream job when he came to America. But, as a result of that non-dream-job, he had saved a significant amount of money and felt pretty good about that. But the inspiring parts of that story are neither the man's career nor the money in the bank; the cabdriver is inspiring because he used his job (literally, the taxi) and his hard-earned money to take care of someone who needed help. Which do you think is more fulfilling—having $10,000 in the bank or rescuing a man from death?

This is what Jesus's story illustrates. A somewhat successful man uses his resources to take care of someone in need. What did the Samaritan do for a living that allowed him to have money enough to take care of the guy who was beaten up by robbers and left for dead? We don't know and we don't care. His career is irrelevant. The Samaritan is a hero because he did whatever it took to love on the bloodied guy in the ditch.

His job and income didn't qualify him to help; his love for his neighbor led him to take action.

Every day, men and women go to work on factory lines or in data-entry positions where they do the same thing over and over for hours at a time—a job they view as a dead end—and dream into the horizon about finding a purposeful and fulfilling career. They dream about what they *could* do for others if they made more money. They dream about what influence they *could* have if they had a certain position or skill set. They dream about the difference they *could* make in issues like poverty, human trafficking, or injustice if they could somehow free themselves from meaningless jobs and trade them in for something meaningful. The opportunities to make a difference presented in the stories above, however, are opportunities that come in any and every setting, regardless of the type of job you have or the amount of money you make.

Today, you will be surrounded by people who are hurting in some way. Today, you will run into someone who is short a few bucks. You may know someone who is trying to overcome an addiction, and they need a friend to keep them accountable or to pick them up late at night when temptation is strongest. You may meet someone recently diagnosed, divorced, abused, widowed . . . And some of these people in need will be people you don't like or who treat you badly. A coworker with whom you don't get along or who has lied about you to others. A gossip or a cheater. He will be the guy who had a bad day and took it out on you for not giving him the discount he wanted. She might look like an angry customer that freaked and chewed you out because her order was wrong. They may be people we see as literal enemies. And God is calling us to be a neighbor to all of them—to love them by meeting their needs and treating them with kindness, especially when they don't deserve it.

Every day, opportunities to love our neighbors are available to us. And this is some really good news for those of us looking for what's next. Today, regardless of what job you have—or while you're waiting for the job you want—you can live out God's calling on your life and find purpose and fulfillment. How? Just look around. Find someone in need and help them.

WHAT'S NEXT

1. Read Romans 13:8–10. How does loving your neighbor fulfill all the other commandments that are listed there?

2. Look around. What are some ways you can make a difference today or tomorrow in someone's life?

12

CALLED TO FREEDOM

A long time ago, there was a really wealthy guy who was also known for his superb moral excellence. He was brilliant in business and very ethical. As a leader, he was responsible for a large group of followers, and I get the sense that he was a "checklist" guy.

I'm guessing he had a checklist for leading people, a checklist for his businesses, and a checklist for morality. He probably knew his net worth down to the penny. He probably kept the lists in a journal and updated them regularly.

The rich leader was always seeking wisdom, and one day he heard about a teacher of religion who was a brilliant thinker and had an answer for everything. He felt he had finally found the guy who could answer one of his biggest questions. In an interesting act of initial humility, this wealthy leader knelt before Jesus as he asked the following question.

"Teacher, what must I do to live forever in heaven and inherit eternal life?"

"You know the commandments," Jesus responded.

- ✓ Do not murder.

- ✓ Do not commit adultery.

- ✓ Do not steal.

- ✓ Do not bear false witness.

- ✓ Do not defraud.

- ✓ Honor your father and mother.

The rich man must have felt a sense of excitement as he mentally checked off the list Jesus gave him. He would have been thrilled that Jesus thought the same way he did. If he's anything like me, he probably smirked with confidence—thinking he had it all together.

"Done! I've done all those things," he reported. "Seriously, I've done all of those things since I was a young boy. Thank you for such great news!"

"Wait a second," Jesus said, stopping the rich man from continuing his celebration. "There's one more thing."

"What is it? What could I possibly lack?"

Jesus looked into the rich leader's eyes. It was obvious that Jesus cared for the man and wanted him to inherit eternal life. Yet, as I imagine was often the case with Jesus, there was a glimpse of something else in His eyes as well: a knowing—a painful knowing. Even the rich ruler began to brace himself for what came next. He could tell Jesus was about to ask for a lot.

Jesus told him, "I see it in your eyes—your money, wealth, and prestige are your gods. You can't worship those things and try to fit the true God in as well. God must be everything to you, and there's only one way you can be free. I want you to go and sell everything you have—including all your land and businesses—and give the money to the poor. After you do that, come follow Me, and you will inherit the true life you seek."

It was a painful moment. Deeply affected by what Jesus had just said, the man felt sick to his stomach.

He wanted to get angry and tell Jesus that there was obviously a misunderstanding. The wealthy man wanted to tell Jesus that He didn't get it—that He just didn't understand and wasn't in touch with the real world. But he could tell from the look in Jesus's eyes that He understood exactly what was going on inside him.

Slowly, the rich leader turned around and walked away in anguish.

INDULGING THE FLESH

This story shows us how the things we truly love—whether it be the pursuit of what's next, a dream job, wealth and prosperity, or a deep desire to matter—can direct us away from God. The rich ruler, whose story is found in Mark 10:17–22, defined his life by wealth and prestige; and his love for money, power, and importance led him away from God. He walked away from Jesus and returned to his life of wealth and influence. His love was misdirected, and it cost him dearly.

But the story of the rich ruler is not included in the Scriptures just so we can both judge and feel sorry for the guy with a misdirected love. I think the story is included in Scripture because all of us have the potential to love something else more than we love God. And if we love something else more than we love God, we could end up doing the same thing—walking away from Him and missing out on the abundant and full life

He has for us. So as you read the rest of this chapter, consider a few questions that this story forces us to wrestle with:

What do you love?

In what ways are your "loves" shaping you?

If you follow your heart, where will you end up?

With whom are you walking?

Wait. What? *With whom am I walking?* What does that have to do with anything?

In chapter 11, I mentioned Paul's quotation of the Second Greatest Common Calling:

> You, my brothers and sisters, were called to be free. But do not use your freedom to indulge the flesh; rather, serve one another humbly in love. For the entire law is fulfilled in keeping this one command: "Love your neighbor as yourself." (Galatians 5:13– 14 NIV)

Paul doesn't end his description of calling there, however, but continues to define God's invitation:

> If you bite and devour each other, watch out or you will be destroyed by each other. So I say, walk by the Spirit, and you will not gratify the desires of the flesh. (vv. 15–16 NIV).

In the story of the rich leader, we see a guy who talked with Jesus—the expert on eternal life—and was invited to follow Him (in other words, *to walk with Him*) and yet *walked away* sad. Why? Because the rich ruler liked the way it felt to have a pocket padded with cash and prestige. If we put that story within the context of Paul's teaching on God's calling, could I suggest that the rich ruler *walked away* from Jesus because he was more concerned with *walking toward* his stuff? Could I take this a step further and suggest that the same temptation—especially as it relates to jobs and career—is in front of us too? Is it possible that we could seek wealth, prestige, and influence and miss God's invitation to true life?

Let's break this passage down a little bit. First, Paul writes that we are "called to be free." What type of freedom do we have? Freedom to be a slave to things that do not bring life, or freedom to experience true life by walking with God. Paul summarizes this idea by contrasting opportunities "to indulge the flesh" with opportunities to love others. Pause. What are opportunities to indulge the flesh? Is he writing to a bunch of cannibals or flesh-eating zombies?

"The flesh" is a term that shows up in the Bible many times. The Greek word here is *sarx*, which, although it means "physical body," can imply much more than just skin and bones. The New Revised Standard Version translates it in this verse as "self-indulgence." The word can indicate someone who is *so* controlled by physical desires that they pursue those desires regardless of the cost to themselves or others. We use various metaphors to describe someone who is pursuing "the flesh" in business: They don't care who they step on as they climb the ladder of success. They will chew people up and spit them out to get ahead. This is exactly the type of thing that Paul is writing to warn against: "If you bite and devour each other, watch out or you will be destroyed by each other" (v. 15).

I don't know about you, but I can already relate to this passage. I know what it feels like to be used. I can look back on one or two bosses and friends—or at least I thought they were friends—who just wanted something I had and couldn't have cared less about me. It doesn't feel good, does it?

If I'm honest—and this one hurts—I can also think of people I've used. I can think of people I've talked to who had something I wanted, and I acted like a friend so I could get it. Any time we look at someone and see only what we can get, we are seeing someone with eyes of "flesh."

As you and I look for what's next in our careers, we will be tempted to follow the cutthroat mentality of our culture. We will be tempted to cut costs and hurt others while padding our own pockets. We will be tempted to look at employees as assets instead of people. To care less about people in other countries than in our own. We will be tempted to lie about the quality of a product so we can sell it. We will point out others' shortcomings while we attempt to make ourselves look superior. There will be opportunities to work long hours at the expense of relationships. We may act as though it all comes down to wealth, prestige, and power. This is what walking in the flesh looks like: only caring about our own success and pleasure and pursuing that success and pleasure at all costs.

That's one option—pursuing self-indulgence or walking in the flesh—but it's not the only option. Paul also suggests that we can (depending which translation you look at) "walk by" or "live by" or "walk in" the Spirit."

WALKING IN THE SPIRIT

Paul defines walking in the Spirit with a metaphor of a fruit-producing plant. Like an apple tree that bears apples or a pear tree that bears pears, someone who walks in the Spirit will produce the fruit of the Spirit. Paul lists that fruit for us in Galatians 5:22–23.

Love
Joy
Peace
Patience
Kindness
Generosity
Faithfulness
Gentleness
Self-control

Paul wants us to understand that when we walk with the Spirit of God, He enables us to step into our calling to freedom—to make the right choices and bear this fruit. In fact, it's only possible to answer God's calling—His invitation—to freedom through the work of the Holy Spirit in our lives. Okay, sounds great. But what does "walk by the Spirit" even mean?

I think it's a lot simpler than it sounds. Remember in the last chapter how both the Middle-Eastern cabdriver and the good Samaritan saw someone who needed help and responded quickly to help them? To the lawyer, Jesus said, "Go and do likewise" (Luke 10:37). That's what it might look like for us to walk in the Spirit. Or what about the misdirected pursuit of wealth at all costs that we just looked at? I recently read a book that encouraged readers that "through intentionally pursuing simplicity and radical generosity we can make an enormous difference" in the world.[1] Walking in the Spirit could show intentional self-control and contentment by not following the latest consumerist trends or fads, and instead looking for any and every opportunity to generously help others—in Jesus's name—with our time and money. If you ask Him, the Spirit will guide you to opportunities to help. Walking with the Spirit could mean hearing His voice, following through on the opportunities to do whatever it is He puts in front of you to do, and giving the Spirit the credit when the person thanks you.

Maybe this will help. The first fruit of the Spirit is *love*. Let's examine love for a moment since loving God and loving others are the big two callings on our lives. There's a section in another one of Paul's letters—1 Corinthians 13—which is famously referred to as "the Love Chapter"—not because it tells you how to find and keep a significant other (although it might work)—but because it defines what love looks like:

> Love is patient; love is kind; love is not envious or boastful or arrogant or rude. It does not insist on its own way; it is not irritable or resentful; it does not rejoice in wrongdoing, but rejoices in the truth. It bears all things, believes all things, hopes all things, endures all things.
>
> Love never ends. (vv. 4–8)

Yikes! Takeaway #1 from this passage? Love is really hard, and I'm really bad at it. Sure, there are times when I'm patient and kind, but all the time? Yeah, right! Ask my wife or kids. About the only aspects of love I've mastered so far are not boasting or being arrogant. I'm really super spectacular at not boasting. Other than that, I'm sunk.

Read those verses again. How are you doing with loving others? Are you ever rude to customers or your boss? Do you ever insist on your own way at work by hiding a cellphone and checking social media instead of giving your job 100% of your effort and energy? Are you ever resentful toward a boss who's treated you—or a friend of yours—unfairly? Have you ever been irritable?

Let's face it—the characteristics of love described above don't come naturally to us. That's why it's so important to realize that love is a product of the Spirit, which means God is the source of our ability to love others. In fact, have you ever noticed the connection between the fruit of the Spirit in Galatians 5 and the characteristics of love found in 1 Corinthians 13?

The fruit of the Spirit	Love . . .
Love	endures all things; never ends
Joy	is not irritable; rejoices in the truth
Peace	does not rejoice in wrongdoing
Patience	is patient
Kindness	is kind; is not rude
Generosity	is not envious; does not insist on its own way
Faithfulness	bears all things; believes all things; hopes all things
Gentleness	is not resentful
Self-control	is not boastful or arrogant

It's not an exact match, but these lists can go together, can't they? And this is really good news because it means that living in the love described in 1 Corinthians 13 is only possible through the work of the Holy Spirit in our lives. In other words, the only way I can love God and love others is if the Holy Spirit does the work in and through me. That takes a lot of pressure off me and you.

And if that were to happen, it would change everything.

Can you imagine what our relationships would look like if

we were able to avoid being rude, arrogant, envious, or boastful? Can you imagine what the world would be like if we Christians were consistently patient, kind, selfless, and hopeful? That would be amazing!

Review the chart above and consider where you are in life right now. Think through your most recent weekday and the opportunities you had to apply the fruit of the Spirit or the qualities of love. Was there a customer who required extra patience? Did you make a mistake and tell your boss the truth about it? Were you kind to a child or a senior citizen? Did you boast about something great you did or try to make everyone envious of your position? Were you arrogant by thinking you're better than a coworker? Were you rude? Did you seek your own interests by skipping work because you wanted to have fun without considering the strain that put on the rest of the staff?

According to Paul, we are called to freedom—we are invited to make a choice—to be led by the Spirit or to walk in the flesh and pursue our own desires. Right now, whatever your position, you have the choice to bear either Spirit-fruit (that sounds kind of weird) or flesh-fruit (that's even weirder). As you look at the future and dream about what God has next for your career, you have the choice to pursue success at all costs or to walk in love. And the best news? You don't have to figure it out or apply this to your life on your own. You have a Helper who walks with you and enables you to discover the full and abundant life the rich ruler missed—the Holy Spirit.

WHAT'S NEXT

1. What are some of the ways you are tempted to "walk in the flesh"? Consider journaling a prayer that chooses the freedom of walking in the Spirit. Invite the Spirit to bear fruit in you beyond what you've ever seen before.

2. When you dream about the future career God has for you, how might the fruit of the Spirit guide those dreams and how you pursue them?

13

UNEXPECTED INGREDIENTS TO SUCCESS

A really long time ago, there was a man named Abram who was called by God to leave his home and his family and travel to a new land. (You may recognize him by the name Abraham, which he was later called.) Although Abram left most of his family behind, his wife, Sarai, and his nephew, Lot, went with him, and they took most of the stuff they owned as well. Now at this time, hotels and moving trucks didn't exist, so Abram, Lot, and their families carried all their belongings on animals. At night they circled up and camped in tents. After what was probably a very long journey, Abram and Lot finally arrived at the land God had chosen for them. But things did not go as planned.

Instead of driving a BMW or owning a house in a gated community, the signs of wealth in ancient times were the size and diversity of someone's flocks and herds. Evidently both

Abram and Lot were quite wealthy because their herds were so large that the herdsmen were getting into fights over whose sheep could graze where. It was kind of like a playground squabble between two "gangs" of elementary school kids: "This is our fort. Go build your own fort over there."

"No! We want this fort!"

"Ms. Cambell, Johnny said we can't play in his fort."

"No I didn't."

"Yes you did!"

I'm guessing the conversation between Lot's herdsmen and Abram's herdsmen was similar! The difference between the herdsmen and the elementary school gangs, however, is that the size of the land on which Abram and Lot were living was not big enough to support all of the animals. The herdsmen were fighting because they were in charge of keeping the animals healthy and well-fed, and it was impossible.

So what does Abram do? Something surprising. He approaches his nephew and says, "Let there be no strife between you and me, and between your herdsmen and my herdsmen, for we are kinsmen. Is not the whole land before you? Separate yourself from me. If you take the left hand, then I will go to the right, or if you take the right hand, then I will go to the left." Abram gave his nephew first dibs on the best land.

The reason Abram's approach is surprising is because Abram was the oldest male, and the leader of the family—something even more significant then than it is now. He had the right to choose whatever land he wanted and could have demanded that Lot move somewhere else. Yet he offered Lot first choice! Remember having to call "shotgun" to sit up front in the car? Now imagine calling the back so someone else could sit up front. Or imagine playing Settlers of Catan and voluntarily giving your stiffest competition—which for me is my wife—the opportunity to choose the first spot. Abram gave Lot first dibs on a choice that had much bigger consequences than sitting in the back of a car or losing a game of Settlers. Herds of livestock were the way a family survived in the ancient world. Livestock meant having food on the table. Abram was setting Lot up for success, while potentially limiting his own success.

Naturally, Lot chose the best land. It had lush green grass and, most importantly, lots of clean, fresh water. The Bible says Lot's land looked like a garden that God made (Genesis 13:10). Did Abram complain? Not one word. He packed up his stuff and moved to a different area so that his nephew, and his nephew's livestock, could thrive.

CHOOSING HUMILITY AND GENTLENESS

In the previous chapter, we discussed the often-cutthroat mentality of our culture, and how the business world, especially, is primed for pursuing success regardless of the cost to others. We contrasted this cutthroat mentality of "the flesh" to life in the Spirit. We looked at how the Holy Spirit is our helper as we look to live out the second greatest common calling and find purpose and fulfillment in loving others.

In this chapter, I want to look at another calling that further expounds on what it looks like to love others. As I hope you will see, Abram's story is a great illustration of how this could play out in your life today, especially as you are searching for what's next. Paul urges us:

> Lead a life worthy of the *calling* to which you have
> been called, with all humility and gentleness, with

patience, bearing with one another in love, making every effort to maintain the unity of the Spirit in the bond of peace. There is one body and one Spirit, just as you were *called* to one hope of your calling, one Lord, one faith, one baptism, one God and Father of all, who is above all and through all and in all. (Ephesians 4:1–6)

As you can see, there are two uses of the word *called* in this passage. The second part of the passage is talking about our first calling—our invitation to salvation through Jesus Christ. That's the calling that we now want to "lead a life worthy of." How can we demonstrate our profound appreciation for God's sacrificial invitation to us? With *all* (some translations say *complete*) humility, gentleness, patience, love—sounds a lot like the fruit of the Spirit from Galatians 5 and the characteristics of love in 1 Corinthians 13, doesn't it?

In the story of Abram and Lot, Abram gave Lot first dibs on choosing land. Abram was entitled to first dibs on where he wanted to settle his family and feed his cattle, but he chose a much more humble and gentle approach.

Think about what could have happened if Abram had exercised his right to choose first and had chosen the land Lot wanted. Put yourself in Lot's shoes. How would you have felt if you were Lot? I'm guessing you would have been ticked off. Just like some of the families I know have split over the distribution of an inheritance or have carried grudges for generations, Lot's relationship with Abram would have been strained at best and potentially permanently splintered. If Abram had chosen first, he and Lot may have never spoken again.

Or what about this. Not only did Abram give Lot first dibs

out of humility, but he also approached Lot with gentleness. Instead of going to Lot and increasing the tension by saying something like, "What's the deal with your herdsmen, dude! Can't you keep your guys under control?" Abram was gentle in his approach: "Hey man! I don't want any problems. I don't want any tension between us. I want to work this out" (Genesis 13:8, author's contemporary paraphrase). I'm reminded of all the times we have to deal with people who are mad at us. Oftentimes, the way we approach them is crucial to whether or not resolution is possible. Paul through his letter and Abram through his example encourage us to approach others with gentleness, especially people with whom there is tension. Sounds like a good way to handle customer service issues, or other sensitive situations that happen in a work setting, doesn't it?

PURSUING UNITY AND PEACE

And here's one more key idea in Paul's words. Look back at the Ephesians passage and circle the words *love, unity, bond,* and *one.* Paul is encouraging the churches in Ephesus to remember that they are all one family in Christ. They are brothers and sisters in the faith, and should pursue "the unity of the Sprit in the bond of peace." Abram did the same thing with Lot. Abram mentions his primary reason for working things out with his nephew: "we are kinsmen" (Genesis 13:8). "We're family, Lot! We can't let stuff like this get in the way of our love for each other!"

Let's pause here for a moment. This is great advice for family or church issues, but what about for issues with people we barely know or don't really care about? How does the call to humility and gentleness apply to a situation where we're in conflict with someone who isn't in our family or faith-circle? What do we do when we have a boss or coworker or employee who is causing problems? How does this apply to tension on a basketball court or in a class? Can we apply this common calling to those situations as well? Absolutely! Because even if the person with whom we are angry is not related to us, and even if they're not a Christian, they are still made in the image of God and loved by God. You and I will never meet a person who is unimportant to God. We are called to look for every opportunity to treat other people the same way God does.

THE PERFECT EXAMPLE

Here's some good news: God is not asking us to do something that He is not also willing to do himself. Look at what Paul wrote on the subject of humility in another letter, and pay attention to the way Jesus is described in this passage:

> So if there is any encouragement in Christ, any comfort from his love, any participation in the Spirit, any affection and sympathy, complete my joy by being of the same mind, having the same love, being in full accord and of one mind. Do nothing from selfish ambition or conceit, but in humility count others more significant than yourselves. Let each of you look not only to his own interests, but also to the interests of others. Have this mind among yourselves, which is yours in Christ Jesus, who, though he was in the form of God, did not count equality with God a thing to be grasped, but emptied himself, by taking the form of a servant, being born

in the likeness of men. And being found in human form, he humbled himself by becoming obedient to the point of death, even death on a cross. (Philippians 2:1–8 ESV)

We are called to be like Christ, who defined humility through His obedience to the Father and His sacrifice for us. Notice these two important points:

- Paul emphasizes unity: having the same mind, same love, and being in one accord with one another. Compare these concepts with the words you circled in Paul's letter to the Ephesians. That's a whole lot of "oneness," isn't it?

- Paul gives us a definition of humility: obedience to God the Father by desiring what's in the best interests of others and then doing it.

Jesus—God's only Son—exemplified humility and gentleness by giving up all His prestige and laying down His life for us. Just like Abram put his nephew first and did not exercise his right to choose the best land, Jesus did not use His entitled position as the Son of God to avoid the opportunity to serve others.

IT'S UP TO YOU

Today, you and I will be faced with opportunities to step into our God-given calling to humility and gentleness, and many of those will come at work. Maybe you work in the service industry and are accused of getting someone's order wrong—instead of jumping into an argument or getting defensive, take the humble and gentle route and simply apologize and make it right.

Or maybe you realize that you've already increased the tension in a situation by not responding with gentleness, patience, and love. You can still make it right, but it's going to take some humility.

Rick Warren writes in *The Purpose-Driven Life*, "Humility is not thinking less of yourself; it is thinking of yourself less."[1] This idea goes against what our culture teaches. We live in a social media world that thrives on thinking about ourselves and pursuing our own interests. We live in a culture that is all about me, my, and I. Yet the calling on our lives, God's will for you and me, is to look out for others before we worry about ourselves. Today, you and I will have many opportunities to think about others and put them first.

Before you get discouraged and think something like, "But if I'm always looking out for others, how will I ever get ahead?" remember this: God's ways are almost always counterintuitive. Look at the conclusion of the stories of both Abram and Jesus. Here's what God said to Abram after he and Lot separated:

> Raise your eyes now, and look from the place where you are, northward and southward and eastward and westward; for all the land that you see I will give to you and to your offspring forever. I will make your offspring like the dust of the earth; so that if one can count the dust of the earth, your offspring also can be counted. Rise up, walk through the length and the breadth of the land, for I will give it to you. (Genesis 13:14–17)

Sounds pretty good, doesn't it? Abram ended up in a much better situation after he put Lot first. He ended up with more land than he ever expected.

Look what happens after the humility of Jesus:

> Therefore God also highly exalted him and gave him the name that is above every name, so that at the name of Jesus every knee should bend, in heaven and on earth and under the earth, and every tongue confess that Jesus Christ is Lord, to the glory of God the Father. (Philippians 2:9–11)

Jesus humbled himself, and God exalted Him to the all-time highest place ever. Of course, things don't always work like they did for Abram and Jesus (and Jesus is God, after all), but Jesus did say, "All who exalt themselves will be humbled, and all who humble themselves will be exalted (Matthew 23:12).

As you look for what's next and maybe work in what you feel is a pointless job, you are in the perfect spot to practice humility and gentleness. If you go to work and give the job your best energy and look for every opportunity to serve others and help them succeed, you will succeed. You will stand out.

If you approach situations of conflict with gentleness—keeping a cool head and showing a smile of kindness regardless of how you feel inside—not only will you experience resolution to most problems, but you will become invaluable to the company. All companies experience conflict both internally (with staff) and externally (with contractors and customers and clients and competitors) and need people who can keep a clear head in a moment of tension. If you're one of those people, they will want to give you more responsibility (and "conflict resolution expert" on a résumé looks really good).

It's almost as if this common calling—the invitation to humility and gentleness—may be a secret to success. So how can you practice humility and gentleness today? Maybe ask this question instead: Who are the people God has put in my life whom I could serve and set up for success? By looking out for them, you just may be setting yourself up for success too.

WHAT'S NEXT

1. Humility is tricky; as soon as you're sure you've mastered it, you've probably lost it. What should humility look like? What does humility look like in your life?

2. Read James 4. Is there anyone with whom you are in conflict? How could you approach them today with a gentle spirit to bring resolution and peace?

14

FIGHT, FIGHT, FIGHT!

He had long brown hair, sported hippy-style glasses, and wore a tie-dye peace shirt. I met him on top of a mountain—well, almost at the top. I was parked at a scenic overlook and was reading my Bible when he walked up to my truck.

"Is the visitor center close to here?" he asked.

"Sure is. Only two more miles and you're there," I responded.

I finished reading and started up my red Chevy to head to work. The man had made it just a hundred yards or so, and I felt like I should offer him a ride.

Four or five legitimate reasons why I shouldn't help immediately came to mind. I didn't want to be late to work. I didn't want to take the chance he'd kill me and steal my truck. You know, things worth thinking about. None of my excuses stuck, however, especially when I thought about how ironic it would be to be robbed and murdered by a guy in a tie-dye peace shirt.

The road was pretty empty, so I pulled up next to him and rolled down the window.

"You want a ride down the mountain?" I asked.

"That would be great!" he answered.

He opened the door and climbed into the passenger seat.

"Were you reading your Bible?" the man asked me.

"Sure was," I said. "By the way, I'm Daniel."

"I'm Beans, and it's nice to meet you."

"Beans?" I asked. "Is that a nickname or your real name?"

"It's a nickname. My dad named me James, but my mom didn't like that name so she called me 'Beans.' I don't really like James either, so I just tell people my name's Beans."

"That's kind of funny. Where are you from?"

"Alabama, originally. That's where I grew up. I'm not homeless, you know. I'm home-free!" he said with a smile.

"What's the difference?"

"Homeless people are those who struggle to find work or have problems that keep them from getting their feet under them," Beans explained. "I'm home-free because I don't want to be tied down. I've actually worked a lot, but I don't want to be bound to a mortgage or anything like that."

I don't want to be bound to a mortgage either, I thought, *but I'd rather have a mortgage than be home-free.*

"I like the Bible," Beans said, bringing the conversation back to where it started. "What were you reading?"

"I was reading about creation and how God put so much of His creativity into the world that mankind doesn't have any excuse not to believe in Him."

"I don't understand how anyone can say there isn't a God," Beans offered. "There's no way you can look at this world and suggest anything other than that someone with a powerful imagination could come up with this place. That's one of the two things that bugs me the most!"

"What's the other thing?" I asked.

"When people try to tell me their religion's the only one. Who are they to say they have it all figured out?"

Normally, when I hear someone say something like that, I search for a way to challenge it. But that didn't feel right in this situation. Something in my spirit—I think it was the Holy Spirit—kept me from stirring up a debate.

"Would you mind taking me to Ingles?" Beans asked, referring to a supermarket in town. "I heard they have great dumpsters. Being home-free is great in regards to bills, but when you travel to a new city—like I am today—and haven't had a chance to work, it can leave you pretty hungry. But you wouldn't believe all the stuff they throw away. One of the guys I know from around here said the Ingles on Tunnel Road is the best one for finding quality food in the dumpsters."

"It's not that far," I replied. "I can take you there."

I gave him a ride to Ingles Market. We talked about creation, God, and the Bible for nearly the entire ten-minute drive. Bean's obvious amazement at God encouraged me, and I think I was able to encourage him a little bit too.

"Thank you for the ride!" Beans said as he got out of the truck. "It was really nice to talk to you."

"You're welcome," I responded.

I'm not sure who was more encouraged from our discussion, but I know that God had set up the entire thing.

If you're like me, you can probably think of a story similar to the one I just shared—a story where you felt like you were supposed to help someone and you actually did it. And maybe, like in my conversation with Beans, you found that helping someone was quite rewarding and encouraging for you too. Unfortunately, if you are like me, you also have quite a few examples of times you felt like you were supposed to help someone but drove away without doing anything. Why is it so much easier to drive away than it is to help? What is the difference—in our mind-set or circumstances or both—between the times we actually help and those times when we drive away? This is a question that keeps me up at night.

In the previous chapter, we discussed what it looks like to put aside our own interests and practice humility and gentleness by lifting up the interests of others. In the chapters before that, we discussed several other common callings that have to do with things like rejoicing always, praying without ceasing, and giving thanks in all circumstances. So many of these callings are invitations to do something or act a certain way, and if we are going to take the common callings of God—the invitations into His will for our lives—seriously, we need to figure out how to do this stuff. Never fear! There's a common calling about that too! I call it the invitation to intentionality.

LIVE WITH INTENTIONALITY

Intentionality is the step beyond good intentions. It's beyond just the desire to help. Most of us have a desire to help those in need. As it relates to this book, most of us *want* to live out God's calling on our lives. But the actual living-it-out part? Now that's hard. In a previous book, *Ten Days Without*, I wrote a lot about people who make a difference in the world versus those who don't. The difference-makers live lives of obedience to God and follow through on their good intentions. It's easy for us to *want* to help someone, but following through and actually helping takes another step—we have to actually do it!

If we're going to apply the things we are learning in this

book—if we are going to live out our faith through obedience to the common callings of God—it's going to take intentionality.

Although most of Paul's letters were written to groups of believers, there are two letters that he wrote to a guy named Timothy—a young man he mentored for many years. Paul wanted to help Timothy navigate some of the more difficult tasks and issues of pastoring churches.

I don't know if you have experienced this yet, but church-life can be complicated! There are specific qualifications for deacons and bishops, questions about false teachings, addressing issues of sin, choosing the color of the carpet, taking care of widows—it's a lot of drama and discipleship and decision-making. Paul didn't leave Timothy on his own to figure it out; instead, Paul spent time with him and then wrote letters to explain critical aspects of church life. Paul ends his first letter to Timothy with a common calling that I think applies to everyone who decides to accept Christ as Lord of his or her life—an invitation to intentionality:

> But as for you, man of God, shun all this. Pursue righteousness, godliness, faith, love, endurance, gentleness. Fight the good fight of the faith; take hold of the eternal life to which you were *called* and for which you made the good confession in the presence of many witnesses." (1 Timothy 6:11–12)

The calling to eternal life is not passive. Paul challenges Timothy to *take hold* of eternal life—to shun (many translations use "flee") certain things, pursue other things, and ultimately fight the good fight of the faith. Imagine Paul standing in the corner of a UFC cage and yelling to Timothy, "Fight, fight, FIGHT!"

First, Paul encourages Timothy to flee some things that are described earlier in the letter:

> Whoever . . . does not agree with the sound words of our Lord Jesus Christ and the teaching that is in accordance with godliness is conceited, understanding nothing, and has a morbid craving for controversy and for disputes about words. From these come envy, dissension, slander, base suspicions, and wrangling among those who are depraved in mind and bereft of the truth, imagining that godliness is a means of gain. Of course, there is great gain in godliness combined with contentment; for we brought nothing into the world, so that we can take nothing out of it; but if we have food and clothing, we will be content with these. But those who want to be rich fall into temptation and are trapped by many senseless and harmful desires that plunge people into ruin and destruction. For the love of money is a root of all kinds of evil, and in their eagerness to be rich some have wandered away from the faith and pierced themselves with many pains. (vv. 3–10)

Paul wants him to run away from false teaching, specifically that which promotes the pursuit of riches and the love of money as if they're forms of godliness. It seems that some religious leaders were using false teaching as a way to get rich. There was obviously a lot of confusion around what it meant to be content and where true contentment comes from. Why would Paul tell Timothy to flee these things? Because he doesn't want Timothy to get anywhere near the types of distractions that may look good or feel good but that ultimately lead to ruin and destruction. He is trying to help Timothy avoid "piercing himself" by making bad decisions that lead to deep pain.

Sometimes running away is a natural response. If you're riding your bike and a pit bull starts barking and running after you, you don't have to think through a desire to flee—you immediately start riding faster! When it comes to false teaching and certain perspectives on money, however, Paul seems to think Timothy might not naturally run away. He may be tempted to listen or to even try out these new ideas. Yet Paul wants Timothy to treat these perspectives on riches and wealth in the same way you and I would treat a ferocious dog. Get away! Get far, far away!

Paul doesn't just tell Timothy to flee certain things, Paul also challenges Timothy to pursue certain things: contentment, righteousness, godliness, faith, love, endurance, and gentleness. In the same way that Timothy won't always run away from false teachings, Timothy may not always pursue what's best either. Again, it takes intentionality to be content, do what's right, pursue the things God pursues, live in faith, show love, endure, and be gentle.

All of this is best summed up in Paul's phrase, "fight the good fight of the faith" (v. 12). I hear Paul saying (insert *Rocky* soundtrack), "Look, Timothy, doing what's right is like a UFC match—it's a fight. You're going to struggle, and you're going to have to choose to do what's right. I want you to *fight!*"

TAKE HOLD OF LIFE

Timothy—and those Timothy was leading—struggled in a culture that defined purpose, fulfillment, and contentment in terms of wealth and prosperity. Sound familiar? As we look for what's next, we will be offered choices similar to that of the rich leader from a few chapters ago—to pursue wealth and prosperity at all costs, even at the cost of the true-life God has for us.

Paul offers an alternative as he instructs Timothy on how to counsel others:

> Command them not to be haughty, or to set their hopes on the uncertainty of riches, but rather on God who richly provides us with everything for our enjoyment. They are to do good, to be rich in good works, generous, and ready to share, thus storing up for themselves the treasure of a good foundation for the future, so that they may take hold of the life that really is life. (vv. 17–19).

Did you see those last three words? That which "really is life."

You and I, like Timothy, are called to take hold of the calling to which we have been called and fight the good fight—to be intentional in choosing to flee the wrong things and pursue the right things, and in so doing to discover true life. In other words, running away may feel like giving up something, but in reality it's finding a better something. So what are some of those right things to pursue? As we look for what's next and pursue not only God's will for today but God's will for our future, what should our lives be about?

The invitation to intentionality—the call to fight the good fight—is incredibly difficult in a job you don't like. You won't want to give this job your best effort. You won't want to wear the uniform. Even if you say "yes" to your boss, inside you might be telling him or her "no!" You will be tempted to use your time at work for your own projects instead of focusing on what's best for the business. You won't care if customers are happy or if the business looks good. In fact, you may want the business to look bad. When you get a paycheck, you will see what you should have made instead of being thankful for what you did make. You will do tasks half-heartedly. You will likely be frustrated—instead of excited—when coworkers get raises or promotions. You may even start blaming your job for bad things that happen outside of work. Or you may blame your current job as the reason you can't figure out what's next or how to get ahead. And when conflict comes up? You won't be thinking about humility or gentleness, you will want to be argumentative and combative, maybe even—dare we say it?—hoping they will fire you so you can move on to something else.

I'm really good at describing the emotions, struggles, and ultimately the symptoms of a job you don't like because I've felt almost all of these at one point or another. Not only that, but I work with people in transition who are looking for what's next, and I can see the face of someone I know and care about in every example I just listed.

In Paul's description of what it looks like to "fight the good fight" he uses a word—*endurance*—that is especially applicable to jobs we don't like. The Greek word means to persevere with patience in all circumstances. Interestingly, it's not the same word that is translated in other places as "long-suffering," but instead implies that someone still has hope because they have a "quality of character which does not allow one to surrender to circumstances or succumb under trial."[1] I can't think of a better way to describe "intentionality." The person has enough character to choose to do what's right, even when circumstances make it difficult to do so.

Today, you will be given the opportunity to fight the good fight—to show the type of endurance that a marathon runner shows at miles 22, 24, and 26 of a marathon—by doing your best in a job you don't like, by doing your best in a class you're not interested in, by doing your best while you're between jobs. Today, you will have opportunities to choose between the temptation to grumble and wallow in self-pity or to ask God for a good attitude to serve the interests of others.

Even in this time of searching for what's next, don't lose sight of God's invitation for *today*—to fight the good fight. Don't miss God's call to flee from the things that drain your life of meaning and purpose, and to take hold of that which "really is life." You *can* do it because the Holy Spirit is with you. Fight the good fight. Be intentional.

WHAT'S NEXT

1. In chapter 13, we looked at Philippians 2:1–8. Read that passage again. What opportunities do you have today to intentionally serve others?

2. Part of living intentionally is seeking justice for others. What could it look like for you to pursue justice? Are there any people you can think of who are treated unfairly? How might you stand up for them?

15

GOD'S SPECIFIC CALLINGS

Although I believe we are all commonly called to the Christlike, Spirit-filled, Father-honoring life and work we've been talking about, and although I think we—both the American culture and the Christian subculture—spend too much time emphasizing the concept of having a specific calling, it's important to acknowledge that God does sometimes call specific people to specific tasks. Besides, you have been reading this book because you want to know what's next for your own life, and you're hoping I have some ideas to help you figure it out. So let's explore some of the biblical examples of specific callings and consider the implications those stories have for us.

That way, if God is calling us to something specific, we have a better chance of recognizing it.

NOAH

Noah was over five hundred years old when God showed up at his door. Well, I don't know if God showed up at his door exactly, but I do know he was really old when God started talking to him about a boat. Interestingly, there's no mention of Noah being afraid when God showed up. It makes me wonder if this wasn't the first time God and Noah talked.

Regardless of the setting, regardless of how it sounded or felt to hear God's voice, if there's one thing I take away from Noah's story, and others like his, it's that most biblical figures were confident it was God speaking to them. There were a few people—like Gideon—who either questioned that it was God speaking to them or wondered if they were actually hearing Him correctly. But for the most part, the Old Testament heroes—people like Noah, Abram, and many others—were so confident that it really was God speaking to them that they simply obeyed when He gave them specific instructions.

> PRINCIPLE #1: WE SHOULD BE ABLE TO RECOGNIZE THAT IT IS GOD DOING THE CALLING.

Even though it didn't make any earthly sense to build the largest boat ever constructed—and to do it in a desert-like climate, no less—Noah obeyed God and did just that. Imagine being at the Grand Canyon and hearing God ask you to build an igloo for thousands of animals because a worldwide ice storm is coming. Noah was in a similar situation, and I can imagine him asking, "You want me to build *what*? Here? What is a boat again?"

It shouldn't surprise us that Noah obeyed, however, because the beginning of the story tells us everything we need to know about Noah and his relationship with God: "Noah was a righteous man, blameless in his generation; Noah walked with God" (Genesis 6:9). The word *walked* has the idea of habit in it—it's what he did all the time. The New International Version says Noah "walked faithfully with God." Think back on our chapter about walking in the Spirit—maybe that's what Noah's life looked like.

I wish I could take credit for realizing that Noah's story was just as much about the way he lived his life before the flood as it was his obedience to God's specific call, but I read it in a book. In his book *Me, Myself, and Bob*, Phil Vischer asks a simple question: "What did Noah do for the first five hundred years of his life?"[1] Genesis 6:9 tells us "he walked faithfully with God."

PRINCIPLE #2: GOD CALLS THE FAITHFUL.

God called Noah to do a specific thing: build a boat and save the world. It wasn't a call to a dream job. God didn't call Noah to a career building boats or working with animals. On the contrary, He called Noah for a specific purpose at a specific time.

But Noah's specific calling was only a small part of his life. His real story is that he walked faithfully with God for more than five centuries. It wasn't until somewhere toward the end of Noah's life that God asked him to do something that would make him the all-time favorite character in children's Bibles. But Noah's life was not just about the specific assignment he received to build a beautiful boat that would later be painted on nursery walls for generations to come and replicated in Kentucky. Noah's life was also about righteousness and faithfulness.

I think Genesis 6:8—"Noah found favor in the sight of the LORD"—might have been what qualified him for his specific calling. In fact, that may be a primary point of Noah's story: God cares about faithfulness.

I think there's a challenge in this story for us too. We have just explored dozens of common callings—invitations from God to live out His will in every area of our lives. As we ask God and wait for His specific calling, maybe we can focus on being like Noah—being faithful in our everyday tasks. On living out God's will, even in what we feel is a go-nowhere-fast job while we wait for something better.

ABRAM

A little later in the Old Testament, we find the story of a guy named Abram (we talked about him in chapter 13). While Noah's story gives us a little context, Abram's starts like this: "Now the Lord said to Abram . . ." (Genesis 12:1). We don't have any clues as to the setting or about the tone of voice God used to talk to him.

From a literary perspective, I think we need to deduct some points. Come on, Moses (many scholars believe Moses wrote Genesis), give us the juicy details! All we know is that God spoke to Abram and called him to do something very specific:

"Go from your country and your kindred and your father's house to the land that I will show you" (12:1).

> **PRINCIPLE #3: WE ARE CALLED NOT NECESSARILY TO A SPECIFIC JOB OR MINISTRY BUT TO A LIFESTYLE.**

Now, it's hard for most of us to understand how big of a deal it was for Abram to obey God's call to leave his home. In those days, families stayed together for lots of reasons, the biggest being safety and support. You know the old adage: "There's safety in numbers." Back then, if you didn't have numbers, your chances of being robbed or taken into slavery were *really* high. Abram was willing to do something you and I can't really understand. But he did it because he was convinced God had specifically called him to leave home and settle in a new land.

Notice that God's call to Abram was not about a dream job or a specific ministry opportunity. God called him to go to a new land where He would provide for him, keep him safe, and create a new nation of people through his bloodline. God's call to Abram was about trust. Do you think God's calling on our lives could be about trust too? If you're trying to discover what's next, you're in the perfect spot to practice trusting God.

> **PRINCIPLE #4: WE ARE CALLED TO TRUST.**

MOSES

We spent a whole chapter talking about Moses, but let's revisit the highlights. Did God call Moses to his dream job? Absolutely not! Moses *hated* the idea of doing what God wanted him to do. Can you think of anyone else in the Bible who used more excuses to try to weasel out of God's specific calling? It's actually pretty entertaining to read the biblical account and consider the excuses Moses used. And then remember his final plea with God? "O my Lord, *please* send someone else" (Exodus 4:13).

> ### PRINCIPLE #5: WE LIKELY WON'T BE CALLED TO A DREAM JOB.

From Moses's story, we learned that God can call some people to do things they don't really want to do. We also noticed that God called Moses to public speaking—something outside of his natural abilities, gifts, and strengths. But the most important part of Moses's story is something you and I can hold on to regardless of what God asks us to do—He will be with us. As we look at Exodus 3, we see how God repeatedly responds to Moses's excuses: I will be with you. I will provide your words. I will help you. That's really good news for us too!

> ### PRINCIPLE #6: IN WHATEVER HE CALLS US TO DO, GOD PROMISES TO BE WITH US.

JONAH

Remember Jonah tried to run away from God and God's specific calling on his life, but God didn't let him get away. In Jonah's story, we see that God's not going to let anyone get in the way of showing love and mercy to people He cares about. In fact, as you and I consider what's next for our lives, we can be confident that God's call will include a heavy dose of showing His love, mercy, and kindness to others.

> PRINCIPLE #7: IT'S PROBABLY
> USELESS TO SAY NO TO GOD
> WHEN HE CALLS US.

MARY & JOSEPH

Although the word *call* is not used in relation to Mary, it's pretty clear that God had a specific plan in mind for her life. It's through her that He fulfilled His promise to send a Savior. Could she have said no to this call? Probably; her words to the messenger found in Luke 1:38 sound like she is agreeing to the plan: "Here am I, the servant of the Lord; let it be with me according to your word."

Since Mary is such an important person in history, you would think she would have some special training or gifts or position and maybe a chapter or two of the New Testament devoted to her. But she has none of those. Have you stopped to think about how little we know about Mary? We know God showed up and said she would get pregnant even though she was a virgin. We know that she responded to that specific calling by praising God and then celebrating with her relative Elizabeth (Luke 1). We know that she believed in Jesus's power because it's her idea for Jesus to provide wine at a wedding banquet (John 2). And we know that she was a witness at Jesus's death (John 19).

Although she accepted this pregnancy as God's "favor" (Luke 1:48) and a "great thing" (v. 49), she was being called to a lot of self-sacrifice.

And what was Joseph—Jesus's earthly dad—called to do? Was he called to be a carpenter and to work with wood and stone? Well, maybe, but that's not mentioned in the few details we have of Joseph's life. We know Joseph was from a town called Bethlehem and that he was from the line of a king named David (Matthew 1:1–18). We know this because he and Mary had to travel to Bethlehem during a census (Luke 2). We know he was a carpenter (Matthew 13:55), and we know he was alive for at least a portion of Jesus's childhood. I think we can safely assume that Joseph was at least culturally religious because he traveled to Jerusalem each year to join the rest of the Israelites in celebrating a major religious festival (Luke 2:41–42). We can also assume that he was Jesus's legal guardian because most of the references to Joseph are attached to Jesus's name like this: "Jesus son of Joseph from Nazareth" (John 1:45).

If we define the word *called* as God summoning us to do something in particular, then we'd have to conclude that Joseph was called to do one thing: protect and raise baby Jesus as His foster dad. First, he was encouraged to marry Mary (Matthew 1:18–25), and then he was clearly directed to protect Jesus by moving the family to Egypt (2:13–18). It seems that Joseph was not called to a specific career but to a specific lifestyle—a lifestyle of faithfulness to God and obedience to whatever He asked of him.

> **PRINCIPLE #8: WE ARE NOT NECESSARILY GIFTED OR QUALIFIED FOR WHAT WE ARE CALLED TO DO.**

Can I just state the obvious here—this was a lot for God to ask of Joseph and Mary!

At that time in history women could be stoned to death for getting pregnant outside of marriage. And by going through with the betrothal, people could have assumed that Joseph slept with Mary before their wedding night. Their obedience to God probably meant a hit against their reputations and probably included more than a few judgmental glances from the neighbors.

In moving to Egypt, Joseph gave up what was likely an established carpentry business for a few years. It also means that they, like Abram had done so many years before, moved away from the support system and safety of family.

> **PRINCIPLE #9: OUR CALL MAY INVOLVE SACRIFICE.**

The story of Joseph and Mary could be a challenge for us too—a challenge to hold things like a successful career, the stability of home, the closeness of friends, and the importance of a reputation loosely. Obeying God could mean sacrificing one or all of those things. It could mean accepting judgmental glances or even accusations as we take care of those God puts in front of us.

Joseph and Mary—two people who don't receive much "Bible-time"—followed the call of God into a life of sacrifice and trust.

SAUL/PAUL

The Saul of the New Testament, it appears, was already doing his dream job when God showed up. He was evidently an excellent Pharisee, and he was very talented at investigating and rooting out threats to Judaism. He seems to have received numerous accolades for his pursuit and persecution of the new Christian church. In fact, if there were a hall of fame for killing and imprisoning Christians, Saul would have been inducted along with a few Roman emperors.

In one of the few New Testament accounts of God's specific calling, Jesus stops Saul in the middle of the road with a light so bright (like LED headlights) that it blinds him for days—long enough that he probably began to wonder if he would ever see again (Acts 9). But God heals Saul and gives him a new name, one that doesn't have all of the baggage attached to it, one that comes with a fresh start. Saul becomes Paul, who becomes one of the most famous leaders in the early church.

Yet even Paul's calling does not include just a specific call to a specific career. Instead, Paul continued to work as a tent-maker in at least one city, and he may have done odd jobs in other cities as well (Acts 18:3). Paul's specific call to planting churches and writing letters of encouragement to Christians around the world was not necessarily a specific call to a career path but a call to a new lifestyle in which Paul used his talents to promote the love and grace of Jesus Christ. And don't forget, Paul's new lifestyle included a whole bunch of suffering. In 2 Corinthians 11 he described the excruciating ways in which he was tortured and abused as a result of his commitment to Jesus. In a way, you could say that Paul was "called to suffer" and we might be too (Philippians 1:12–30).

> PRINCIPLE #10: OUR CALL IS FOR
> GOD'S GLORY, NOT OUR OWN.

I share all of these examples because they have all challenged my view on God's calling. When I was younger, I assumed that God's call was to a specific job, yet in many biblical stories, God's calling is outside of what the person does for a living. And in each case, some aspect of God's character is shown through what the individual is called to do—God's love, mercy, kindness, compassion, grace. Most of the biblical examples describe men and women of character who were far from perfect but lived lifestyles of faithfulness to God.

> PRINCIPLE #11: WHAT WE
> ARE CALLED TO DO WILL
> DEMONSTRATE GOD'S CHARACTER
> TO OTHERS.

I think our obedience to the many *common* callings of God in our lives is the precursor to, and may be more important than, the *specific* calling of God. And if we believe God might be calling us to do something specific, we should consider these stories as we analyze what we believe He is calling us to do.

Here's the thing: until you and I can answer all the questions below with a no-holds-barred "yes!" searching for a dream job or God's specific calling to a career is just a distraction from what the Bible heroes of old demonstrated through their lives and sacrifices. First and foremost, they were men and women of character who walked with God and were obedient to God. If God has a specific thing for you to do, He'll show up and make it clear, just like He did for them. Until then, living with character and faithfulness is the challenge for us too! Check out these questions. Can you answer "yes" or do you—like me—have some work to do?

- Do you talk to God daily?
- Are you willing to trust God with every aspect of your life?
- Do you obey what you already know to do from Scripture, the common callings?
- Do you actively try to show God's love, mercy, and compassion to others?

WHAT'S NEXT

1. Read Matthew 11:28–30. How can you respond to this invitation? Does following God feel "easy and light?"

2. Read the story of Gideon in Judges 6:11–7:22. What do you observe about God's call of Gideon that could be principles that help us understand how God calls people?

16

NOTHING WASTED

In the past ten years, I graduated from college, worked six different full-time jobs and a few part-time jobs, and graduated from seminary. I was a sales associate at a bookstore, a bartender at a country club, the director of marketing for a family entertainment center, the director of content and marketing for a small nonprofit, a radio producer for a nationally syndicated radio program, and the general manager of a family entertainment center and restaurant. If this list of jobs seems somewhat random to you, I can affirm that it *felt* random as I moved from job to job and opportunity to opportunity. Yet what was random to me was not random to God.

One of the primary lessons I've learned is that God doesn't waste experience. God is able to use even the worst situations for good. Proverbs 16:9 puts it this way: "The human mind plans the way, but the LORD directs the steps." Isaiah says it slightly differently: "When you turn to the right or when you turn to the left, your ears shall hear a word behind you, saying,

'[Hey, *your name.*] This is the way; walk in it!'" (30:21). And Paul puts it this way: "We know that all things work together for good for those who love God, who are called according to his purpose" (Romans 8:28). What I think we see in these passages is not that God tells us exactly what to do all the time, but that He is guiding us even when it doesn't feel like it.

I graduated from college with a degree in hospitality and tourism management—a degree I didn't want and tried to get away from a few times—and yet I've spent much of my life, unexpectedly, in that field. When I worked for the nonprofit, I started a blog that led to my first book. That first book was a nightmare in so many ways; do you remember the story I shared with you about being fired in Michigan? Well, what I didn't tell you was that the day before I was let go, the book opened up the door for me to meet a guy named John. John interviewed me about the book for a social media website. A few years later, he became the marketing director for a publisher in Michigan and helped open the door for me to write a second book. God used a bad job experience and an unexpected setback to arrange a meeting with the guy who later helped me launch a new direction in my career. God was directing my steps (Proverbs 16:9) and using even bad situations for my good (Romans 8:28).

My first book was also the reason I was offered a job at the nationally syndicated radio program. Although I had no radio experience—zero, nada, zilch—the hiring manager said, "If you can write a book, you can produce a program." Again, God was using a bad experience for my good.

A subsequent radio interview about my second book opened up the door for more conversations about the potential of joining that radio program—*Discover the Word*—on a permanent basis. Guess what experience I was able to list on my résumé when I started trying out for *Discover the Word*? My previous job as a nationally syndicated radio producer. Again, God was weaving seemingly unrelated experiences together for good.

Why am I sharing all of this with you? Because although I'm just now getting to the point where I really enjoy my career, I could *never* have pulled all of this together on my own. Ten years ago, I had no idea I would like radio work or writing books. When I look at my "random" work experiences, I can see how God used every single job to prepare me for the next step, and the next step, to where I am today. I tried to plan my way, but it was undoubtedly God who directed my steps. I turned to the right and the left, but it was God's still small voice behind me saying, "Hey, Daniel! Come this way."

As you read the rest of this chapter and consider helpful tools for discovering what's next, please don't lose sight of your very Good Father who's working things out for your good. You may feel like you're in a horrible, no good, very bad job (especially if your name is Alexander), but God is going to use that experience to shape and guide you into what's next. You may feel like God isn't being very helpful right now, but I'm confident that one day you will look back on today with a new perspective. I think you will see that God was with you and at work in directing your steps.

Now to the tools! In case I haven't made it clear enough yet, none of these will provide perfect, one-time, clear-cut answers. But the more you experience and explore, the more clarity you may find, especially as you continue to pray each step of the way!

TRY IT ON FOR SIZE

I once heard someone say that the best way to figure out what you like to do is to try a bunch of different things. For some of us, this means jumping from job to job. For others, it might mean picking up a hobby or two. For me, it meant reading lots of books.

I met my wife in high school, and we got married halfway through college. When I started to wonder what career to choose, I couldn't afford to try out different career options because I already had the responsibility of supporting a family. So instead I read about different careers and the people who did those jobs full time. Find people you know who work in areas that interest you and ask them about their experiences. What do they like? What don't they like?

Make a list of what interests you. Make a second list of what doesn't interest you. Use those lists as you consider your options.

TAKE TESTS

There are a bajillion careers out there—at least that's how it feels. It can be overwhelming to decide which jobs to try out. One of the ways to narrow down your options is to take a strengths test. I prefer CliftonStrengths, which I use for new team members who join our staff. Personality tests are also really useful; tests like the Enneagram and DISC help you understand your own strengths and weaknesses in the workplace and in getting along with others. Those mentioned here are not free, but many others are available online for free.

Knowing what you're good at and how you work best with

others is not a guaranteed way to discover what's next (remember Moses?), but if you're deciding between two different jobs or career fields, knowing what you're naturally inclined to can be helpful in deciding which to choose. And the results of these tests have a way of putting words to things that otherwise it might take you years to figure out about yourself.

FIND A MENTOR

Another helpful tool is using the experience of and leaning on the wisdom of someone older who is further down the road of life. Why learn from your own experience if you can save time and heartache by learning from someone else's? The right mentor won't tell you what to do but will ask the right questions to help guide you to your own conclusions.

God directed me to a mentor. I was struggling with trying to discover what was next and had been asking God for help. I was in a series of meetings when one particular guy walked in the door and I felt the Holy Spirit say, "Daniel, get to know that guy." I don't know how else to describe it. That night, I emailed the guy and asked if he'd meet me for coffee. I shared with him what had happened and asked if he'd be my mentor. Somehow that didn't scare him away, and we've been hanging out for enough years now that I've lost count. If you are looking for someone to talk with, who has the wisdom to back up his or her advice, pray and ask God to provide someone.

NEVER QUIT ASKING QUESTIONS

Another way to discover what's next is to ask yourself—and others—questions. Lots of them. Questions can get the creative juices flowing as you begin to dream about what God has for you. Here are some ideas for questions to ask yourself and others:

> Is there anything you would do for free just because you enjoy it that much? (My buddy Michael roasts coffee and bakes homemade bread all the time. I'm pretty sure that's going to be a part of his future one day.)
>
> If money and experience didn't matter, what career would you choose?
>
> What do you read about in your free time because it interests you? (Remember my college buddy Ben whom I caught studying personal finance books even though he wasn't taking any classes on finance?)
>
> If you can remember being a kid, what were some of the dreams you had back then, before you became a realist?
>
> What gives you joy?
>
> What steals your joy?
>
> What do you like and dislike about your current job?

Here are some more questions to ask yourself:

> Are there any activities that when you do them, you light up and feel God's pleasure? The famous runner Eric Liddell once said (at least in the movie *Chariots of Fire*), "I believe God made me for a purpose, but He also made me fast. And when I run I feel His pleasure." For me, I love teaching, especially the Bible. I don't care if it's to three people or five hundred—I enjoy

taking things I've learned and passing them on to others. What's your passion? When do you feel God's pleasure?

Are there any repeated themes to the encouragement other people offer you? For example, do people who know you say things like, "You have a pastor's heart" or "Wow! You're really good with numbers"?

What are you good at?

What are the jobs and careers that you can rule out completely? Why?

Are you a people person or do you like jobs that you can complete alone?

What opportunities are *actually* available to you?

What is your life's mission? What do you want to accomplish? What job could fit within this mission?

Again, the point of these questions is to help get creativity flowing through your heart, soul, mind, and strength. Use the answers to start more conversations with God, your mentor, and your boss!

FIGURE OUT WHAT YOU'RE ABOUT

The last question mentions your "life's mission." For some, this may be a weird idea, but it's something I've found helpful. A friend of mine named Andy Andrews wrote a blog about writing your own personal mission statement.[1] If you google his name and "personal mission statement" it will come up. Here's why it could be helpful.

A few months ago, Jeff Manion from Ada Bible Church in Grand Rapids was being interviewed on *Discover the Word*, and he made one comment in particular that has stuck with me. He suggested that knowing your mission is important because it opens the door for "a confident yes and a liberating no." All of the tools we've looked at in this chapter should be leading us to "a confident yes and a liberating no." They should help us say yes to things that fit within what God has for us to do, and to say no to things that are just a distraction from God's mission for our lives. There are so many jobs out there. There are so many good causes. There are so many service opportunities and places to donate money. How can you navigate all of those options? By knowing what your life is about—knowing your strengths and abilities, listening closely to God—so you can say "yes" with confidence to the right opportunities, and say "no" to *good* options that aren't what's *best* for you.

REMEMBER: THE NEXT DECISION IS NOT YOUR FINAL DECISION

Here is one last helpful concept that was passed on to me by one of my previous pastors: your next decision is not necessarily a final decision. A few years ago, I was trying to decide between two job options—to become a pastor at a church or to move back to North Carolina and become the general manager of a family entertainment center and restaurant. It was a stressful decision, and I felt like Robert Frost looking at two roads diverging in a yellow wood and doubting that I would ever come back to this crossroads again. It felt permanent. It felt like saying yes to one option meant saying no to the other, forever. I had the same feeling when I was trying to choose a major in college.

I was sharing this anxiety with my friend and pastor, Ken, and I will never forget what he said to me: "Saying yes to one option doesn't mean that you will never get the chance to do the other option. Today, say yes to whichever one you feel God is leading you toward. In a few years, the other option might come back around too. You have a lot of life in front of you, and God's not done directing your steps. I don't think this decision will be your final decision as it relates to your career."

There are so many times when a decision will feel absolutely final—as if there's no way we can get out of it. For some of us, it's the choice between two jobs. For others, it's a choice between two or three different majors. What is your choice?

Take heart, my friend. Saying yes is not as final as it may feel. Trust God, follow Him where you feel He is leading and trust that He will bring other opportunities at the right time. A decision today is not necessarily a decision for tomorrow.

A FINAL WORD: REDEFINING SUCCESS

I have a friend who lives in Rwanda. His name is Dan, and he and his wife are incredible people. He's one of those guys you meet and immediately feel like you've known forever. Do you know someone like that? Someone who makes you feel right at home? Someone you can joke around with and who gets your style of humor? Someone who is excited to invite you over to his or her home even though you just met ten minutes earlier?

I had spent just a few minutes with Dan as he helped our team exchange money before I knew that if we had any downtime later in the trip, I wanted to spend some of it with him. At the end of the week, my wife and I and another friend named Justin had a day off. We called Dan, who then came and picked us up and took us to an excellent coffee shop (I knew I liked this guy). If you're not a coffee drinker, you may not realize that quite a bit of coffee is grown in Rwanda. So I'm not being cliché when I tell you this was really, really fresh coffee. It really was an excellent coffee shop!

We were all interested in Dan's experience as a missionary,

and much of the conversation consisted of one-sided questions as we picked his brain. One question in particular led to an answer that has stuck with me: "Dan, what is the biggest lesson you've learned in your time here in Rwanda?" I asked.

He didn't hesitate with his response.

"I've learned to redefine success," he explained. "When we moved here, I was caught up in how to prove to our supporters back home that their money was well spent. I needed to prove to them that our ministry was effective, and I began to search for ways to quantify our influence. Unfortunately, ministry here was very slow, and there weren't any good measurables to point to and say, 'See, here's the difference we're making in Rwanda.' At first, I was ready to abandon the ministry. It obviously wasn't working. But God had a different idea.

"God began to show me that success is not defined by the numbers of people we can influence, but it is defined by our faithfulness to do whatever God has placed in front of us to do. It's not about how many people we influence, but about whether or not we influence the people God brings our way. It's not about the number of sermons I preach, but about my faithfulness to research, pray through, and deliver each sermon that God provides.

"And if we do that—if we define our success here in Rwanda by our faithfulness to do whatever God asks us to do—we will not only be effective in our ministry but we can also be at peace knowing that we walked with God and obeyed Him. After all, isn't that really all that matters?"

As we consider the wisdom of my friend Dan, may we learn what it means to walk faithfully with the God we love enough to worship Him with our lives. May our definitions of success in life be defined not by the quality of our jobs, by the amount of money we make, or by the number of people we influence. But instead, may we define success by our faithfulness to do whatever God places in front of us to do today. And may we not be overly concerned with discovering a specific call or dream job, but instead with faithfully obeying the many common callings the Bible teaches.

With God's help, we can.

ACKNOWLEDGMENTS

Thank you . . .

If you read this book and you're now reading the Acknowledgements, I'm blown away! Who does that? You rock! I'll try to make it fun. In fact, I want to mention you first. To you, the reader, there are a gazillion books to choose from, and I'm so thankful you gave this one a chance. I'd love to hear from you. Visit danielryanday.com and connect with me using the options at the top of my page.

Books are like bobsleds—it takes a team to drive it down the mountain. "Feel the rhythm, feel the rhyme, get on up, it's bobsled time" (quote from Disney's *Cool Runnings*).

God. *What's Next* is, at its core, a book that describes what God has been trying to get me to understand for many years—that He loves me and directs my steps. That I don't have to worry about what's next, because He's already there and has plenty for me to focus on here, now, and today. Thank you, Father, for answering my prayer and helping us (me and Dawn, my editor) put this book together.

Rebecca, my love—this book wouldn't exist without your patience and support. Love you, babe!

Thank you, kiddos! Without your distractions, this book would have been finished earlier. Thank you for your constant prayers, and for sitting on my lap, or on my shoulders, or under my feet while I put this book together.

Mom and Dad—you gave me a space to try out these ideas. Granny and Jimmy—you both inspire me, and I love you.

Thank you, Blythe Daniel—my secret agent friend—and the Blythe Daniel (Secret Agent) Agency for believing in this project and helping me put together a great proposal.

A few very special friends: Dr. Meg Meeker, Robert Brenner, Andy Andrews, Michael and Emily Erb, Bishop Ken Ross, Rev. Kenneth Robertson, Lynn Ray, Debbie Medford, Hambone, Ryan, Correy, Neisa, Dean, Roger, Christy, Nick, Joe, Joanna, Diana, Dustin, and Doyle.

Finally, I want to thank the team at Discovery House and Our Daily Bread Ministries. I want to especially thank y'all for believing in this content so much that you gave it a second book. And Dawn, thank you for pushing back and helping the *Intentional Christian* content become so much more accessible for a new batch of readers. Also, thanks to Mart, Elisa, Bill, and Brian—*Discover the Word* has changed the way I read the Bible, and I hope I honored the team in the way I handled the Scriptures in this book. Thank you all for your help and support!

NOTES

CHAPTER 6

1. Bruce Waltke, *Finding the Will of God: A Pagan Notion?* (Grand Rapids, MI: Eerdmans, 1995), 7–8.

CHAPTER 10

1. Information on the *Sh'ma* was compiled from the following sources: Christopher J. H. Wright, *Deuteronomy*, Understanding the Bible Commentary Series (Grand Rapids: Baker, 2009); "One Lord, One Love, One Loyalty (Deut. 6:4–25)" The Bible Study App; and Bruce K. Waltke, *An Old Testament Theology* (Grand Rapids: Zondervan, 2007), 484.

CHAPTER 11

1. Darrell L. Bock, *Luke*, The IVP New Testament Commentary Series (Downers Grove, IL: InterVarsity Press Academic, 1994), 199.

CHAPTER 12

1. Ian Morgan Cron, *Chasing Francis: A Pilgrim's Tale* (Grand Rapids: Zondervan, 2013) kindle, 242.

CHAPTER 13

1. Rick Warren, *The Purpose-Driven Life* (Grand Rapids, Zondervan: 2002), 148.

CHAPTER 14

1. *Complete Word Study Dictionary: New Testament*, ed. Spiros Zodhiates (Chattanooga, TN: AMG: 2013) sv. "5281. ὑπομονή hupomonḗ," Olive Tree Bible App.

CHAPTER 15

1. Phil Vischer, *Me, Myself, and Bob: A Grown-Up Book about God, Dreams, and Talking Vegetables* (Nashville: Thomas Nelson, 2006), 242.

CHAPTER 16

1. Andy Andrews, "The Ultimate Guide to Writing Your Own Personal Mission Statement" Andy's Blog and Podcast, March 10, 2016, www.andyandrews.com/personal-misson-statement.

To inquire about having Daniel speak at your church, school, conference, or event, please email connect@intentionalchristianity.com or connect via social media:

danielryanday.com
facebook.com/danielryanday
twitter.com/danielryanday

Enjoy this book? Help us get the word out!

Share a link to the book or
mention it on social media

Write a review on your blog, on a retailer site,
or on our website (dhp.org)

Pick up another copy to share with someone

Recommend this book for your
church, book club, or small group

Follow Discovery House on
social media and join the discussion

Contact us to share your thoughts:

 @discoveryhouse    @DiscoveryHouse

Discovery House
P.O. Box 3566
Grand Rapids, MI 49501 USA

Phone: 1-800-653-8333
Email: books@dhp.org
Web: dhp.org